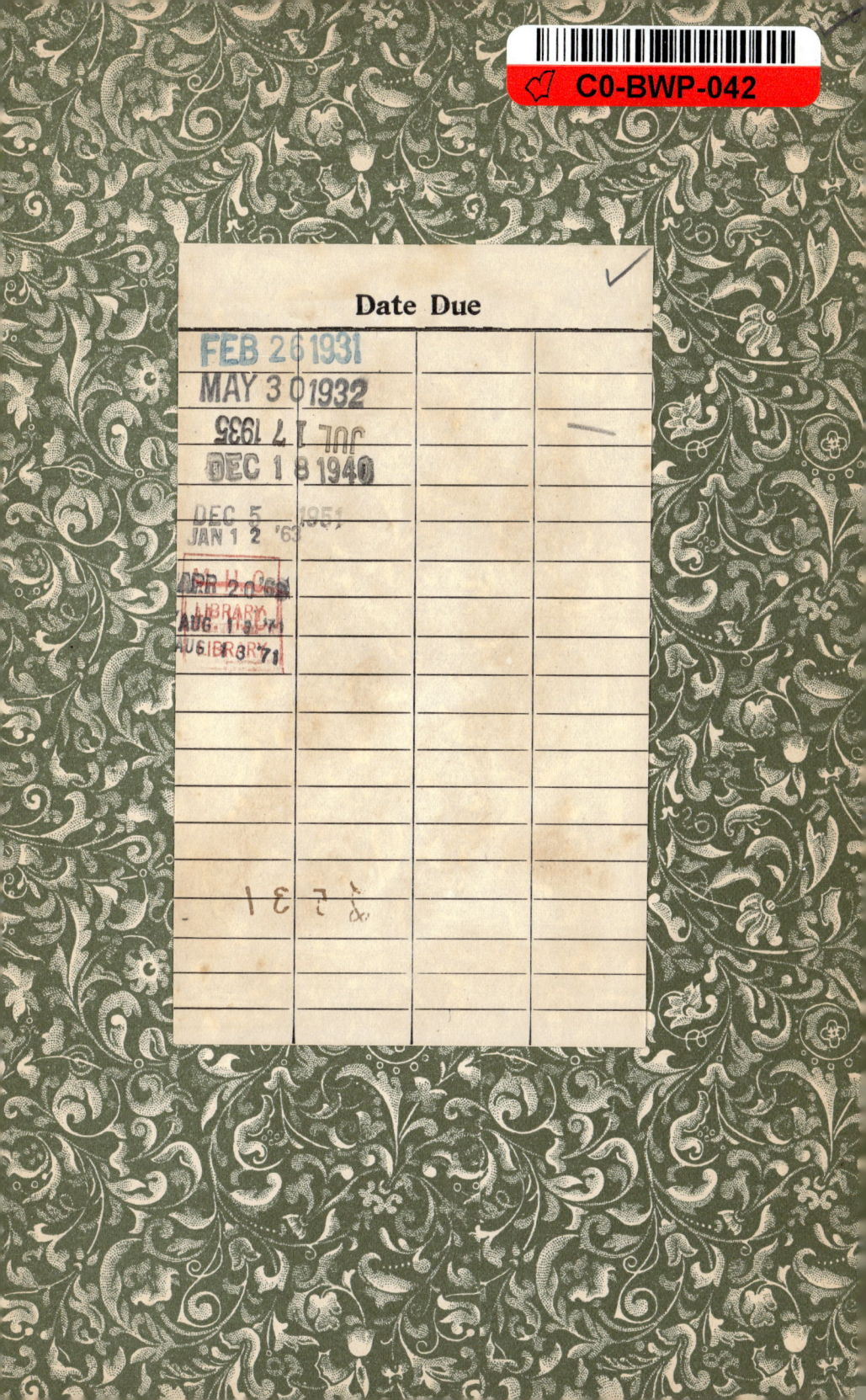

Please do not take out of the Library.

PROPERTY OF
MORRIS HARVEY COLLEGE
LIBRARY

DISCARD

COST CAPITALIZATION

AND

ESTIMATED VALUE

OF

AMERICAN RAILWAYS

AN ANALYSIS OF CURRENT FALLACIES

BY

SLASON THOMPSON
BUREAU OF RAILWAY NEWS

THIRD EDITION

CHICAGO:
GUNTHORP-WARREN PRINTING COMPANY
1908

385
T37c

2531

NOTE.

Except as they present facts and legitimate deductions. no authoritative value is claimed for these pages. Neither is any railway official or organization responsible for the views expressed herein. They are published by the writer as the result of four years' study, in which he has had time and opportunity to investigate the subject beyond what was possible in his many years of active daily journalism.

Wherever statements of fact are not matters of common knowledge their source is given. From these facts only the most obvious deductions have been drawn.

S. T.

Chicago, 1907.

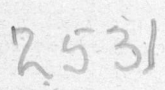

There can, indeed, be no doubt that American railways are less over-capitalized now than they have ever previously been, the amount of profit diverted to capital purposes in recent years having been on a truly colossal scale.—*London Statist*, August 24, 1907.

CONCLUSIONS BY WAY OF PREFACE

From the facts presented in the following pages it is submitted that the VALUE of railway property in the United States employed in the service of the public is shown by several independent methods of inquiry to exceed their total NET CAPITALIZATION.

Historically, the cost is shown to be always cumulative, while the capitalization has sometimes been scaled down and millions of expenditures have never been capitalized.

Where the NET CAPITALIZATION in 1906 has been officially declared to be only $11,671,940,649, the cost or value ascertained, through several processes, is approximated as follows:

CONSTRUCTION AND EQUIPMENT to June 30th, 1905, $13,000,000,000
   (Exclusive of appreciation of right of way and terminal rights.)

COMMERCIAL VALUE, as approximated by Prof.
   Henry C. Adams as of June 30th, 1904........$11,244,852,000
Applying Prof. Adams' formulae to earnings of
   1905 ....$15,235,765,167
Applying Prof. Adams' formulae to earnings of
   1906 ....$17,248,620,000

MARKET VALUE as shown in quotations of securities, anywhere

From $11,000,000,000
To $14,000,000,000
                                         and upward,

according as affected by politics, crops, value of money and manipulation.

By COMPARISON with capitalization of foreign roads

From ....$13,384,240,000 (on the Canadian basis)
To ....$21,969,000,000 (on the German basis)
or ....$28,712,000,000 (on the French basis)
or ....$34,795,000,000 (on the Belgian basis)
or ....$58,644,000,000 (on the English basis)

Even allowing $100,000.00 per mile for the difference in the value of right of way (the only feature of cost greater in Great Britain), American Railways capitalized on the English basis might fairly be capitalized at $37,000,000,000 and with freight rates as charged in England their commercial value on Prof. Adams' theory would exceed that amount.

On the basis adopted by Japan in the purchase of private roads of Japan, in 1906, the value of American Railways on the average business of 1904, 1905 and 1906 would be over $14,505,000,000.

Capitalized according to the price paid by Japan for the inferior railways of Japan, the value of American Railways would be nearly $16,000,000,000

And finally:

On the ratio of assessed value to the true value of all property in the United States, as reported by the Federal Census Bureau, the assessment of American Railways for the purposes of taxation is a certificate of value for $12,890,000,000, or **over a billion dollars more than their Net Capitalization.**

INTRODUCTION

Why Official Valuation of Railway Property is Desirable

In numerous official and unofficial utterances, President Roosevelt has made it clear that he has lent a more or less complaisant ear to the theorists and agitators who for many years have been clamoring for government valuation of the property of the railways of the United States represented by their stocks and bonds. This clamor was put in concrete shape in the amendment to the Hepburn Act introduced by Senator La Follette, which reads:

"That the Commission shall estimate and ascertain the fair value of the property of every railroad engaged in interstate commerce, as defined in this act, and used by it for the convenience of the public."

That the demand thus formulated was not original with the senator from Wisconsin is proven by the discussion of its practicability by Professor Henry C. Adams in his first report as Statistician to the Interstate Commerce Commission for the year ending June 30, 1888. In this he asked: "Is it possible to discover the cost and value of the carrier's property, franchises and equipment?" And while he was of opinion that such a task was a "prodigious," if not an impossible one, he thought that a trustworthy estimate of the relation existing between "the present worth of railroad property and its cost to those who are proprietors of it" might be obtained. He also thought that "the estimate of social agitators on the one hand and of men interested in the present status on the other might be far from the truth."

The idea present in the mind of Statistician, Senator and President is, and always has been, that the cost or capital of railways exercised a controlling influence on rates. In other words that the falsely alleged "exorbitant rates" on American railways were due to the necessity of paying interest and dividends on gross over-capitalization.

It has gone for naught with the "social agitators," back of this contention, that the rates on American railways are not exorbitant, being the lowest in the world. Neither have they been able to grasp the truth that rates are not fixed by dividends, because they close their understanding absolutely to the mute immutable testimony of such figures as the following, showing that while gross railway capitalization per mile has steadily increased during the period of Mr. Adams' incumbency of his present office, the tendency of average rates has, almost invariably, been downward:

GROSS CAPITAL AND AVERAGE RECEIPTS PER MILE, 1888-1906.

Year.	Gross Railway Capital per Mile.	Passenger Receipts per Passenger Mile (Cents).	Freight Receipts per Ton Mile (Cents).
1888	$56,498	2.349	1.001
1889	56,892	2.165	.922
1890	58,659	2.142	.941
1891	59,006	2.126	.895
1892	61,130	2.108	.898
1893	59,729	2.111	.879
1894	59,419	1.986	.860
1895	59,650	2.040	.839
1896	59,610	2.019	.806
1897	59,620	2.022	.798
1898	60,343	1.973	.753
1899	60,556	1.978	.724
1900	61,490	2.003	.729
1901	61,531	2.013	.750
1902	62,301	1.986	.757
1903	63,186	2.006	.763
1904	64,265	2.006	.780
1905	65,926	1.962	.766
1906	67,936	2.002	.748

Here is an official demonstration that while the capitalization of American railways increased $11,438 per mile between 1888 and 1906 their average passenger receipts per mile declined more than a third of a cent, and their freight earnings per ton were less by over a quarter of a cent per mile.

President Roosevelt and Senator La Follette and Professor Adams and all intelligent students of railway affairs understand the significance of these figures, but the "social agitators" dwell upon the increase of capital and never tell their deluded followers that a reduction of one-third of a cent per passenger mile on the traffic of 1906 meant a saving of $87,000,000 to the traveling public, while a decline of 2.53 mills in the rate per ton mile meant a loss to the railways of $545,974,000 on the freight traffic of 1906.

These two items make a total greater by $138,000,000 than the aggregate of interest and net dividends paid by the railways in 1905. In other words the possible net profits of the railways in 1906 were practically cut in two by the decline in passenger and freight rates between 1888 and 1906.

Any relation between capitalization and rates such as is harped on by the "social agitators" is thus demonstrated to be an iridescent bubble proceeding from more "water" on the brain than there is in all the railways in the universe.

The prevalence of such popular hallucinations, however, emphasizes the necessity for an intelligent attempt on the part of the government to ascertain and publish to the world a reasonably trustworthy estimate of the cost and true valuation of the railways of the United States. The right to regulate carries with it the duty to protect. This was recognized in the passage of the original Act to Regulate Commerce and by the first Commissioners appointed under that act. In its first report written by the late Judge Thomas M. Cooley, than whom no higher authority ever wrote on railway subjects, the Commission says:

"The act to regulate commerce was not passed to injure any interests, but to conserve and protect. It had for its object to regulate a vast business according to the requirements of justice."

The power to decree reasonable rates carries with it the duty to preserve the property of the railways from confiscation or unreasonable rates, and the Supreme Court of the United States has declared that a railway company "is entitled to ask a fair return upon the value of that which it employs for the public convenience." Furthermore, it has decided that:

"In order to ascertain that value, the original cost of construction, the amount expended in permanent improvements, the amount and market value of its bonds and stock, the present as compared with the original cost of construction, the probable earning capacity of the property under particular rates prescribed by statute, and the sum required to meet operating expenses, are all matters for consideration, and are to be given such weight as may be just and right in each case."

If it were established once for all, under the stamp of an impartial investigation, that the ascertained value of the railways after due consideration of these elements was equal to or exceeded the sum of their stocks and bonds, very much of the popular hostility to their management would disappear. Such hostility is undoubtedly fanned into radical demands for restrictive and oppressive legislation by the reiterated charges that extortionate rates are imposed in order to pay profits on excessive capitalization. Nothing short of a thorough governmental investigation of the cost and value of the property used for its convenience will satisfy the public who are right, the "social agitators" or the hundreds of thousands of American citizens who have invested billions in American railways.

Unless it can be shown, that the cost or present value of the railways approaches their capitalization, the crusade of the "social agitators" will continue to attract followers by confusing cries of "water" and "over-capitalization" in one breath and "exorbitant rates" and "discrimination" in another. This too in spite of the testimony of such an unprejudiced expert as Chairman Martin A. Knapp of the Interstate Commerce Commission, who as long ago as 1899 testified before the Industrial Commission as follows:

"I have not seen any instances in which the rates have seemed to much depend upon or be influenced by the capitalization of a road.

"Q. You have never seen such a case?

"A. I have not. The capitalization of the railroad, I think, cuts no figure in this rate question."

This from a firm believer in the principle that "a fair valuation on the railroad properties" is an essential basis for a judicial determination of what the proper rate should be, would seem to be conclusive.

It is therefore as a measure to protect their rights in any judicial investigation into their rates, that I would recommend to the railways that instead of opposing they should insist upon an official valuation of their properties. Such a valuation by an intelligent and fair-minded commission, would, in my opinion, result in a convincing demonstration that American railways, as a whole, are under-capitalized, and that all the "water" that from time to time has been present in their stocks has been absorbed by the cost of improvements, plowed back, as the farmers say, into them from operating expenses and net earnings.

Given such a Commission as that named by Governor La Follette himself, which has recently made a report on passenger rates in Wisconsin, remarkable for its comprehensive thoroughness and judicial fairness, and the railways have nothing to fear but much to gain by supporting Senator La Follette's proposition, so far as it relates to the valuation of their properties. If there ever was a case of a man smitten dumb by a granted prayer, it would be the Senator from Wisconsin by the report of any commission capable of making a reasonably adequate and just valuation of railway properties in the United States.

The only thing the railways have to fear is the appointment of prejudiced or incapable appraisers.

It is the purpose of the present writer to anticipate, so far as may be, the findings of such an official body, conceding at the outset that anything like an authoritative valuation of railway property is beyond the reach of his expectancy. Even the government with all its resources and inquisitorial powers can never arrive at a definitive conclusion of what has been well called a "superhuman task."

The difficulties confronting such an undertaking are practically insuperable. That of numbering the stars deals with more tangible units. As the Railway and Warehouse Commission of Minnesota, which has essayed the task for a single state, admits, it involves "the closest personal examination of all the physical properties of each company doing business in this state." Moreover those entrusted with it must be (to quote from the same authority) "Men of wide experience, who thoroughly understand the business in all its details, and who know the values of everything which enters into the problem, from the right of way to the completed road, with all its necessary equipment. As every line has its own physical obstacles to overcome and the necessary conditions of efficiency and the necessary equipment in each case involves nearly every circumstance affecting the business, such work cannot be hurriedly or superficially done without complete sacrifice of the value and usefulness of the work as evidence."

Then the Commission enumerates a few of the items comprised in its investigation as follows:

"The detailed examination into the present value of lands for right of way, yards and terminals; the cost of tracks, bridges, buildings, shops, machinery and tools, engine-houses and turntables, locomotives, freight and passenger cars, in fact, every item that enters into the physical property of the railroads of the state."

It must be evident that when the value of all these things have been estimated—they cannot possibly be ascertained—there remain the intangible rights and opportunities to be guessed.

What this may amount to can be "guessed" from the fact that the Tax Commission of Texas in 1906 valued the intangible properties of the railways of that state at $152,827,760 after deducting $188,600,939, the value of their physical property fixed by the Railroad Commission, "from the true cash value of all the property of said companies" in Texas.

No guess based on earnings can be admitted, being precluded by the purpose of the inquiry to find "a safe foundation upon which to construct fair and reasonable rates," for the rates are themselves the determining factor in the earnings.

Nothing short of omniscience can know or find out what the State of Minnesota has undertaken in the premises.

Manifestly, therefore, nothing absolutely conclusive will be attempted or should be expected in these pages. But it is believed that by applying various tests with candor and common sense a more or less convincing estimate of the present value of railway property in the United States, as a whole, may be arrived at. Statistics will be used only to aid ordinary intelligence to reach a sane conclusion.

To begin with, comparison will be invited to measure the cost and capitalization of American railways by that of foreign railways. This test involves a very simple process and would be of great assistance if the physical and financial conditions of railway construction and the necessities of traffic in different countries could be reduced to a common basis for comparisons. Unfortunately this is impossible and therefore comparison, "the right hand of logic," will only be appealed to to throw a sidelight on the subject.

Next there is the historical method of investigation. This will trace the making of American railways from the small beginnings three-quarters of a century ago and their gradual evolution from the twenty-three miles of horse power railways in 1830 to the 317,083 miles of all kinds of track in 1906. Done with any approach to exhaustiveness this would require as many volumes as the "Messages and Papers of the Presidents," which will never be brought up to date. But no commensurate estimate of the cost and value of American railways can be made without at least a cursory review of the trackless task that confronted them, and the various stages of their development. "The Winning of the West" by the voyageur and pack train has no more stirring stories of courage, adventure and indomitable energy than can be found in the final conquest of this continent by the surveying parties, construction gangs and steam horses of railway history. And all along the trail of almost incredible achievement there has been one continuous chorus of pessimism and detraction. Criticism and speculation between them have made the construction of American railways an undertaking beset with quicksands and whirlpools. The history of railway construction as written in Wall Street has been one thing; its history in the field, from the driving of the first spike by one of the signers of the Declaration of Independence, down to the present day, has been another.

Unfortunately, the financiering of railway companies has received more attention in public prints than the details of the expenditures involved in making the railways themselves. Coups in Wall Street by which the control over the properties was seized or shifted, have obscured the unsensational progress by which those properties were steadily and often stealthily transformed from the "strap rail" period to vast transportation systems of today. And so we are left to guess what this transformation cost, and are forced to piece out any information we have of original cost by an inquiry into what it would cost to produce existing railways at present prices. Thousands and millions of dollars have gone into the making of the railways of America which is represented in the properties but not in the capitalization of present companies. Panics, abandonments and reorganizations have dealt cruelly with the investments of thousands who put their faith in the alluring railway prospectuses of the past. The public has been the only invariable winner throughout the record of experiments, wrecks and receiverships that mark the financial history of American railways. It has been truly said that no matter how unprofitable any particular undertaking has been to its owners, no American railway has failed to bring profit, sometimes ten fold, to the community it served. This is true although there are thousands of miles of badly located roads in the union which never should have been built where they were first surveyed. Once built, however, the investment in them has been irrevocable, and the years come and go without bringing the balsam of dividends to cure the original mistake.

It is the futility of attempting to get at the original cost and subsequent sums poured into sustenance, as well as maintenance and improvement that has brought most economists to consider that the present value of railways can best be approximated by the cost of reproduction at present prices. The investment of foresight, energy and spirit of venture, to which we owe the railways as much as to the actual money invested, may be considered as being represented by the increase that has come in the value of the right of way and terminals, to which the railways have contributed their value.

While it is doubtful if the present cost of reproduction new would cover the original cost of the railways, plus the cost of reconstruction concealed in yearly and daily maintenance and improvements to meet the ever increasing traffic, it is generally admitted that no other method would so nearly and justly recognize all the elements that underlie the present value of American railways. And after the cost of reproduction is estimated there remain other elements of value to be considered, notably that intangible, illusive thing known as franchise value. This is a possession of the railways which may have more value than their tangible property and yet there is no known method by which that value can be estimated with any approach to convincing accuracy. It is more nearly represented in net earnings than anywhere else. The right to operate over a favorably located line in a territory of dense traffic between termini of increasing originating or distributing potentialities, is the possession that differentiates successful railways from the failures. The physical attributes are the mere means for its exploitation.

Such an inquiry as this must include an estimate of the commercial value of the railways as a system. This means the market estimate of the property, not according to its cost or its value as a physical proposition, but as based on its net income and what is termed the "strategic significance" of the property. In 1900 in response to a Senate resolution the Interstate Commerce Commission made one approximation and in 1905 Statistician Adams of the Commission made another appraisal for the Census Bureau. Both of these are interesting but unconvincing contributions to the study of the subject.

Another means of arriving at an estimate of the value of railways is to study them through the returns of the different assessors and state boards of equalization. Here they are weighed in scales which have never been tipped in the favor of the corporations to any notorious extent. When it is considered that they are regulated as public highways, the levying of any tax upon railways is an anomalous proceeding. But in the matter of taxation the railways are treated as private corporations and pay taxes in excess pro rata of those paid by the tillers of the soil, the manufacturers and the merchants whom they serve at the lowest rates on earth.

Through these various mediums, which in some instances overlap and afford cumulative testimony, it is thought an approach may be made to a convincing estimate of the present value of the railways of the United States—at least sufficiently convincing to dissipate from all reasonable minds the impression that as a whole American railways are grossly over-capitalized.

Nothing authoritative will be attempted in this inquiry, its only aim being to present facts that will enable the fair minded to arrive at a mean estimate of the value of our railways that shall approximate the truth. This, it is believed, will support the view of President Hadley of Yale that "the effect of a fair valuation would be overwhelming proof of the reasonableness of American railway rates as fixed at present."

I

A SEVEN BILLION DOLLAR ERROR

The Reductio Ad Absurdum

In approaching a subject of such infinite possibilities for error, it is well at the outset to sweep aside the one obvious misstatement which from its bold reiteration may be regarded as the chief corner stone of the present agitation against American railways.

In his three-day speech before the Senate on April 19, 20, and 23, 1906, Senator La Follette having, on the estimates of one reckless writer, estimated that in 1903 there was seven billion dollars of water in the capital of American roads, took occasion to adopt the theories of another even less reliable author to astound his hearers with the statement that $8,000,000,000 odd of their capitalization in 1904 was entirely fictitious.

It is interesting to trace how Senator La Follete worked himself up to this magnificent absurdity. In 1893 Mr. Van Oss of London published a work entitled "American Railways as Investments," which, with true insular abandon, fairly reeked with charges of fraud, dishonesty and recklessness in the construction and financiering of American railways. As a result of Mr. Van Oss' alleged investigations, to quote Senator La Follette's words, he arrived at "two important conclusions:

"First, that the average amount originally received in actual value for American railway bonds probably did not exceed 67 per cent;

"Second, that the original investor in American railway stocks certainly paid not more, on the average, than 10 per cent. of their face value, and probably less."

Then Senator La Follette, accepting these glaring fictions as facts, on his own account went on to construct he following Eiffel tower of error:

"If an estimate of the actual investment on American railroads is computed on the basis of these final percentages given by Mr. Van Oss on the capitalization of 1904, as reported by the Interstate Commerce Commission, we get the following result:

Senator La Follette's Estimate.

Stocks, 10 per cent of $6,339,899,329, say	$ 65,000,000
Bonds, 67 per cent of $6,873,225,350, say	4,585,000,000
Total investment represented by $13,213,124,679, total capital....	$4,650,000,000
Or say...	$5,000,000,000

"The remaining $8,000,000,000 odd are entirely fictitious capitalization, and cannot be considered in discussion of railway earnings."

Why Senator La Follette made the mistake of saying that $65,000,000 was a round figure for 10 per cent. of six billion odd, or did not swell his fictitious capitalization to eight and a half billion, as he well might by the showing of his original error, is not explained in the context in the Congressional Record.

That Senator La Follette was thoroughly possessed and fascinated by the false estimates cited in this speech is proved by the following extract from his speech of May 18, 1906, explaining his vote on the Hepburn bill:

"So long as the legislation relative to the common carriers of this country permits these corporations to increase their capital stock without limit, increase it without adding anything of value to their properties, and increase it solely with the purpose of fixing rates upon that inflated capitalization, in order to pay profits and dividends to those holding the stocks and bonds, in which they have no real investments, just so long this question will be a vital issue before the American people. There is today in the stock and bond valuation of the railroads of this country **upward of seven billions of water.**"

Let us examine this fictitious Niagara in the light of incontrovertible facts:

According to the last statistical report of the Interstate Commerce Commission, the total railway capital outstanding, including stocks, bonds, income bonds, equipment trust obligations, and miscellaneous obligations was $14,570,421,478. Of this $2,257,175,799 stock and $641,305,030 bonds was owned by the railways in their corporate capacity and was not in the hands of the public, and in the language of the official statistician, "to the extent that such reductions are proper, overstates the capital." This leaves the net capital of the railways at $11,671,940,649.

There are certain physical appurtenances to the operation of railways which have a standard average value, namely, locomotives, cars, rails and ties. They cannot be bought for "water."

Their cost as they stood on June 30, 1906, may be tabulated thus:

ESTIMATED COST OF EQUIPMENT, RAILS AND TIES.

Items.	Cost.
51,672 Locomotives at $12,000	$ 620,064,000
42,262 Passenger Cars at $6,000	253,572,000
1,837,914 Freight Cars at $1,000	1,837,914,000
78,736 Work Cars at $600	47,241,600
*309,218 Miles of Track, 70-lb. Rail, at $28 per ton	1,066,802,000
Ties for ditto, 2,880 to the Mile, at 50 ct.	445,273,000
Total	$4,270,866,000

*Estimated.

This affords the basis for the following demonstration of the absurdity of Senator La Follette's claim that there is "upward of seven billions of water" in the stock and bond valuation of the railroads of this country today:

DEMONSTRATION OF SENATOR LA FOLLETTE'S ERROR.

Net Capitalization in 1905 (official)	$11,671,940,649
Cost of five items, as above	4,270,866,000
Balance	$7,401,074,049
Senator La Follette's "water"	7,000,000,000
Balance to represent the "upward"	$401,074,049
Capital available for all other construction of 309,218 miles of track	00,000,000,000

As it would cost more than $30,000,000 for spikes, irrespective of other fastenings, to attach the rails to the ties on

309,218 miles of track, and more than $625,000,000 for the ballast in which to imbed the ties, there can be no possible escape from the *reductio ad absurdum*.

When one considers that the six items in the above table of cost merely represent the superstructure and ephemera of railways (and not all of these), which have to be continually renewed and replaced or they become defective or obsolete, amazement grows at the magnitude of Senator La Follette's error. Nowhere does the table include the real thing—the location, right of way, strategic position, grading, cuts, fills, bridges, tunnels, stations, freight houses, shops and other properties and rights that make the railway the highway upon which the traffic of a mighty people moves with ever-increasing volume and despatch. These constitute from two-thirds to three-fourths of the value of the property of the railways used for the service of the American public today. Unlike the items in the table, right of way and location of railways are not subject to depreciation, but increase in value with each passing year with the increase in population and wealth of the United States.

It is well for the Senator that the rule *falsus in uno, falsus in omnibus* does not apply to all senatorial utterances.

II

WATER IN RAILWAY CAPITAL

Nothing has served so continuously to darken counsel in regard to American railways as the glib charge that they impose extortionate rates in order to pay dividends on watered stock. It flows with equal fluidity from the lips of economist, agitator and demagogue, and it has been thus flowing so long that it has been accepted as true by a majority of the American people. In truth, it has ever been mostly a theory, never a general condition.

Now, what is this "water" in railway capital which is the subject of such popular opprobrium?

Generally speaking it is used as a synonym for fictitious capitalization—meaning that either stock or bonds or both have been issued for which no equivalent was paid, or is represented, and that the value of the property is not equal to the face value of these obligations. In this obvious sense its use is noted in financial literature early in the seventies and it is first recognized by Webster in his 1879 Supplement as "Brokers' Cant."

In the Century Dictionary it is classed as "commercial slang," and is defined as follows:

"To increase the nominal capital of a corporation by the issue of new shares without a corresponding increase of actual capital. Justification for such a transaction is usually sought by claiming that the property and franchises have increased in value so that an increase of stock is necessary in order to fairly represent existing capital."

Legal writers define watered stock as a security issued as fully paid in, when, in fact, the whole amount of the par value thereof has not been paid in.

Under both of these definitions it will be perceived that there may be legitimate and illegitimate watering of railway capital. But the term has been so persistently and offensively abused by critics and commentators, as well as detractors of American railways, that the distinction is lost in popular discussions of the subject. The public has been led to believe that the increases in railway capitalization during the past thirty years have been largely fictitious; that they have been made to conceal large dividends on stock, and to forestall the demands for a reduction in rates.

It matters little to the parties whose chief capital is denunciation of watered stocks that, water or no water, the increase in net railway capitalization from about $7,000,000,000 to $11,671,940,649 during the past twenty years has been accompanied by a reduction of freight rates from 1.04 cents to 7.48 mills per ton mile and of passenger rates from 2.19 cents to 2.002 per passenger mile. They will continue to cry "Water, water, everywhere!" in hopes that the discovery of a few cesspools in railway finance will convince the public that all sources of railway capitalization are polluted at the fountain head.

Senator La Follette is not the only advocate of a valuation of American railways who professes to think that they are floating islands surrounded by oceans of water. Only last winter the Washington correspondent of one of our great dailies wrote to his paper that:

"Every development of late shows that most of the big lines of railroads in the United States are vastly over-capitalized, some of them having a funded debt and capital stock issues amounting to from two to ten times their actual cost."

The point of this watery delusion was put thus: "It is easy to see that if a railroad has been capitalized at a figure five or ten times its value it must meet a fixed charge five or ten times as great as it should be expected to meet."

It will be observed that "actual cost" and "value" are here used as interchangeable terms and the illegitimate water in most of the big lines was said to be from 50 to 90 per cent.

To well-informed readers the mere extravagance of such a statement carries with it its own refutation. But to the suspicious, the prejudiced and the ignorant there is nothing incredible about the most palpable and self-stultifying exaggeration. If Senator La Follette could carry off a seven billion dollar misrepresentation without question in the United States Senate, why should anyone hesitate to believe a statement that for one part of cost there are nine parts of "water" in the capitalization of American railways?

Neither must it be thought that this cry of "water" is any modern invention! In one form or another it has been a continuous chorus which has accompanied the floating of every railway enterprise since Colonel Stevens first sought to raise funds to construct a railway from the Delaware River to the Raritan in 1815. Every government or corporation issuing securities and selling them at a discount, whether at 90 per cent., as the German Empire has within six months, or at 50 cents on the dollar, as some of the early American railways had to, has watered its capital stock to that extent. In his letter of August 24, 1897, classifying the items to be charged to cost of construction, Statistician Adams recognized its legitimacy in these words: "To this account should be charged discount on securities sold; interest on loans affected, and on notes issued for construction purposes or overdue payments to contractors or other creditors, and discount, interest and exchange on other commercial paper issued for a similar purpose."

When the first railway was built in the United States, money in a perfectly safe investment commanded 10 per cent. and upward. Neither then nor at any time since has railway construction appealed to investors as a perfectly safe investment. At the start, national, state and local authorities doubted its financial success more seriously than its practicability. They had absolutely nothing upon which to base a favorable judgment. Such assistance as they were finally induced to extend to the pioneer railways was in the nature of subsidies, land grants or guarantees, to encourage an experiment in transportation rather than an investment made with any hope or expectation of a monetary return. How railways were regarded in those days is well reflected in the report of a special Board of Commissioners to the Pennsylvania legislature in 1831:

"While the board avow themselves favorable to railroads where it is impracticable to construct canals, or under some peculiar circumstances, they cannot forbear expressing their opinion, that the advocates of railroads generally have overrated their comparative value. The board believe that notwithstanding all the improvements that have been made in railroads and locomotives, it will be found that canals are from two to two and a half times better than railroads for the purposes required of them by Pennsylvania. And they again repeat that their remarks flow from no hostility to railroads, for next to canals they are the best means that have been devised to cheapen transportation."

In the beginning not only in New England and in some of the Southern States, as we are generally told, but throughout the Union, roads were largely built with money raised by the sale of stocks, and it was upon the security of these original investments and the rights thus secured that money was borrowed on bonds for their completion. In these cases shareholders were induced to subscribe on favorable terms that promised more than the then current rate of interest on their money. Paid-up stock was issued at 75, 50 or even 25 cents on the dollar, according as the risk was great or slight, or the returns promised to be immediate or remote. The building of a road to connect centers of population and established trade relations had manifest elements of profitable traffic absolutely absent from the majority of railway enterprises that quickly engaged the speculative enthusiasm of that generation of railway projectors.

American investors were quick to appreciate the difference between investments in railway bonds and railway stocks. They recognized that the stocks represented, as one writer (A. M. Wellington) puts it, "the risk only, the dubious margin which is dependent upon sagacity, skill and good management," while the bonds represented "a certain minimum value," for which the property and all its hereditaments and potentialities were pledged. Upon this simple distinction grew up the practice of "sweetening" the sale of bonds with bonuses of stock. Bonds carrying 6 to 8 per cent. would be sold with different amounts of stock thrown in as a premium, the bond purchaser feeling sure of a share in the property in any event and being tempted to make the investment by the prospect of higher returns on the stock.

With many of the projected roads it was a case of "woodchuck or no meat." Their projectors simply were forced to give bonuses with the bonds, sell the bonds at a heavy discount, make bricks without straw, or leave the roads unbuilt until some less conservative parties came along who had the faith and confidence that move mountains and build empires through the combination of capital and wisely directed energy.

From 1830 down to this day there has never been a time when the "sagacity, skill and good management" ever active, dominant and progressive in American railways, has not more than made up for any excess of nominal capital over capital actually paid in and expended on the property. But whether this be admitted or not, there is abundant evidence in the cost of the railways themselves that the par value of their capital in dollars and cents derived from some source has been expended upon them.

For three-quarters of a century the managers of American railways have followed the sound financial policy of reinvesting undivided profits in their properties. In lean years and fat alike this course has been pursued. Even when in the stress of hard times there have been no net profits and some roads have been thrown into receiverships, the process of enrichment has gone on with the proceeds of receivers' certificates, which, with returning solvency, have gone to swell the funded obligations of the railroads.

That the shareholders in American railways are entitled to be credited with the gross sum of these undivided profits turned back into the property as well as for all expenditures for betterments, improvements and excess of cost of renewals, is admitted by every economist who has given the subject sober thought. The principle is precisely the same as that by which the thrifty individual instead of spending all he makes or earns invests a percentage of it to extend his business. The abstinence from distributing all the net earnings of railways among their hundreds of thousands of stockholders,* which is distinctively

(*)   The last official report put the number at 327,851.

an American policy, represents one of the factors in the creation of wealth which has always been recognized by economists. In this case it accounts for the comparatively low capitalization of American railways in contrast to the British practice which has been to distribute all the net profits and charge all betterments and improvements to capital account. The low capitalization of American railways is due to the policy tersely expressed in the phrase, "A dollar for dividends and a dollar for betterments."

Because the official statistics are confused by including the returns from non-operating railways,—which are in no sense legitimate subjects of interstate regulation, neither are they common carriers, for they carry nothing,—it is impracticable to give anything like a complete summary of the moneys expended annually by the railways on additions, betterments and improvements. In the year 1906, however, the returns made to the Interstate Commerce Commission by 313 operating roads showed that 94 per cent. of the railways of the United States devoted no less than

$$\$220,316,034$$

of their income to improvements "charged to income account," "other deductions" not chargeable to the operations of the year and in surplus. The income account of these roads in 1906, considered as a system, may be summarized as follows:

Income Account, 1906

(206,960 Miles of Line Represented.)

Earnings from operation...		$2,246,421,166
Expenses of operation..		1,482,148,334
Net earnings...		$764,272,832
Less taxes..		67,356,217
Earnings less taxes...		$696,916,615
Charges:		
Interest on funded debt..........................	$252,572,777	
Interest on current liabilities..................	13,819,287	
Interest on real estate mortgages................	422,322	
Rent leased lines................................	116,144,978	$382,959,364
Balance available for dividends, adjustments and improvements.......................		$313,957,251
Dividends—Common................................	$175,334,923	
Preferred..	46,005,909	
Other payments...................................	166,371	$221,507,203
Balance..		$92,450,048
Deficits in operation of 76 unprofitable roads...................		12,292,750
Net balance from operation......................................		$80,157,498
Income from other sources.......................................		140,158,136
Balance available for improvements..............................		$220,316,034
Disposition of balance:		
Improvements charged to income...................	$56,502,413	
Other deductions.................................	59,610,904	
Surplus..	104,202,717	$220,316,034

The income from other sources is principally derived from rentals and from railway stocks and bonds owned by these operating roads, and practically takes care of the rents and interest charges on the debt incurred in the purchase of such securities. If these items of income and expense could be eliminated, the balance for improvements would not be materially affected.

During the past sixteen years the official statistics show the following balances "available for adjustments and improvements," the sums under "permanent improvements" being included in the total sum available in comparison with the net dividends in each year:

INVESTMENTS IN IMPROVEMENTS FROM INCOME DURING SIXTEEN
YEARS 1890-1905.

Year.	For Permanent Improvements.	Available for Improvement and Adjustments.	Net Dividends.
1905	$37,720,624	$185,088,372	$188,175,151
1904	38,522,548	143,691,430	183,754,236
1903	41,948,183	190,856,993	166,176,586
1902	34,712,968	172,977,856	157,215,380
1901	31,938,901	150,392,692	131,626,672
1900	25,500,035	142,754,358	118,624,409
1899	13,070,045	92,719,113	94,273,796
1898	6,847,905	78,370,389	83,995,384
1897	4,544,813	20,300,720	(1) 87,377,989
1896	5,162,240	26,525,485	88,097,757
1895	4,016,382	(2) 1,001,805	85,961,500
1894	4,418,003	(3) 16,821,274	101,607,264
1893	2,957,069	37,045,024	102,941,289
1892	4,126,273	45,499,874	101,929,135
1891	4,887,975	40,721,296	96,489,013
1890	4,511,508	41,765,491	89,688,204
Total	$264,885,472	$1,289,709,898	$1,877,933,765

(1) Dividends previous to 1897 inclusive are swelled by duplications.
(2) There was a deficit after paying for permanent improvements.
(3) Deficit.

Notwithstanding the fact that prior to 1897 the dividends were swelled by duplications amounting to at least $12,000,000 annually—in 1897 the exact figures were $12,245,480—it will be perceived that the undivided profits of the railways devoted to their betterment amounted to over three-fourths of the sum distributed in dividends. Nor does this showing, impressive as it is, tell the whole truth, for in the years 1894, 1895 and 1897 in addition to the figures shown in the table the railways had to account for deficits of unprofitable roads amounting to $45,851,294, $29,845,241 and $6,120,483, respectively.

During the years covered by the foregoing table the total amount of capital stock outstanding not owned by railway corporations has increased from $3,445,804,726 to $4,484,504,943 or $1,038,700,217, which is almost exactly a quarter of a billion ($251,009,681) less than the aggregate sum retained from the stockholders and devoted to the betterment of the property in that period.

It is out of such persevering, constructive, progressive, American financiering as this that the railways have been nourished by "water" into the admirable position of the lowest capitalized high standard railways in the world.

And mark you, this does not complete the tale of their enrichment at the expense of the stockholders. In the year 1906, the 313 roads above mentioned expended on road and equipment $14,593,642 which was included in operating expenses, exclusive of expenditures in certain cases amounting to less than $100 on road, $300 on equipment, and not taking account of excess of weight of rails and improved quality in renewals on some of the largest systems in the country. This sum is equivalent to $70 per mile of line. Accepting this as an average, and it is a low one, the railways of the United States in thirty years between 1875 and 1905 have paid over $300,000,000 for improvements and charged it to operating expenses. Does anyone seriously question that this is a legitimate investment of money belonging to stockholders?

Between 1850 and 1900 the improved farm lands in the United States increased from 113 to 414 million acres, or considerably less than fourfold. In the meantime the value of all farm property increased from $3,967,343,580 to $20,439,901,164, or more than fivefold. The average value per acre of all farms has risen from $13.50 in 1850 to $25 in 1900, making a difference of over $8,000,000,000 in the wealth of American farmers, compared with what it would have been at the prices of fifty years ago. Would anyone call this vast accretion of wealth "water" because chiefly due to the railways and not represented by any equivalent capital invested in farms, except out of surplus earnings?

Each generation of railway critics has found some particular American road to single out as the terrible example of overcapitalization. It used to be the Erie. Now it is the Chicago and Alton Railway that is the target of this unenviable notoriety. Twenty-six years ago the Chicago and Alton's total capital account, covering 840 miles of main line, was $37,821,727 or $45,239 per mile. If divided by the miles of all tracks it was equal to $35,629, and President Blackstone frequently claimed that the Alton was capitalized at only 60 per cent. of its accumulated cost. Twenty-six years ago its disbursements on account of funded debt, rent and dividends amounted to $2,624,446, or nearly 7 per cent. on its total capital account, which covered the leased lines.

Last year the capital liabilities of the Chicago and Alton were $119,046,218, or $122,728 per mile of line, or $83,658 per mile of all tracks. The reader will perceive that the capital per mile of line had been nearly trebled while per mile of track it had been only slightly more than doubled.

Such are the incomplete facts coupled with sensational stories of fortunes made through manipulations that have filled the press with a perfect deluge of charges of "water." These it is not necessary to discuss now. Here it is sufficient to say that the total annual disbursements on account of this gross capitalization foots up $3,468,528, or 2.92 per cent Moreover, these capital disbursements in 1906 amounted to only $2,347 per mile of track, where the like disbursements in 1880 amounted to $2,473, and in 1870 to $3,028 per mile of track laid with 56 to 65 lb. **iron** rails.

Paradoxical as it must seem to the economists of the hydropathic school, the increased capitalization of the Chicago and Alton has been attended by a remarkable decline in the rates paid by the public both for passengers and freight, as the following statement shows:

	PERIODS OF		
	Low Capital.		High Capital.
	1874 (a) Cents.	1880. Cents.	1906. Cents.
Passenger receipts per mile.................	3.267	2.076	2.05
Freight receipts per ton per mile............	2.123	1.206	0.639

(a) Passenger and ton mile units first available for 1874.

Evidently the "water" in the Chicago and Alton, like the paints of the master artist, must have been "mixed with brains" to produce such results, and its patrons, if not the "social agitators," have reason to await the next shower with equanimity.

It was Judge Thomas M. Cooley who first directed attention to the danger of arousing popular hostility against railway management because great private fortunes had been amassed in their control. "The natural conclusion," he said, in his first report as chairman of the Interstate Commerce Commission, "which one draws who must judge from surface appearances is, that these fortunes are unfairly acquired at the expense of the public; that they represent excessive charges on railroad business, or unfair employment of inside privileges, and furnish in themselves conclusive evidence that current rates are wrong and probably extortionate. An impression of this sort, when it happens to be wide of the fact, is for many reasons unfortunate. It creates or strengthens a prejudice against all railroad management—the honest as well as the dishonest—which affects the public view of all railroad questions; it renders it more difficult to deal with such questions calmly and dispassionately; it makes the public restive under the charges they are subjected to, even though they be moderate and necessary; it tends to strengthen a feeling among the unthinking that capital represents extortion. However careful, considerate, fair and just the management of any particular road may be, and however closely it may confine itself to its legitimate business, it is impossible that it should wholly escape the ill effects of this prejudice, which are visited upon all roads because some conspicuous railroad managers have by their misconduct given in the public mind a character to all."

Throughout every period of the development of American railways, economists, theorists and agitators have been so intent on watching the black spots on the system as revealed in Wall Street speculations and financial crises that they have overlooked its underlying sanity and solvency. Even such an eminent authority as Charles Francis Adams failed to properly emphasize the fact that it was overconstruction and not overcapitalization that brought about the financial disasters of the seventies. He recognized that "the mania for construction, which began in 1866 and culminated in the crash of 1873," had outstripped the business needs of the country, but he reserved his severest criticism for the gross scandals that disgraced the management of some of the companies. Morally he was right, and no strictures could be too harsh for the jobbery that prevailed in railway speculation. But through the worst of it the railways of the country went steadily forward, some with water and some without, giving the American people constantly improved service at constantly declining rates.

Then as now the railways were entitled to be judged by their general performances and not by the misdeeds of their black sheep. In the very heat and stress of the Granger movement, when the railway companies were compared with the feudal barons as levying iniquitous taxes upon the commerce of the country, they were not paying extravagent profits on cost of construction, they were not over-capitalized and the rates charged to shippers had been steadily declining for three decades.

In 1873 the railways of the United States were over-constructed but not over-capitalized. Today they are both under-constructed and under-capitalized, but the facts have been so misrepresented that the springs of fresh capital are dried up by popular and legislative hostility. A year ago the railways were in a position to borrow money for much needed improvements and extensions upon reasonable terms. Today they are forced to abandon their extensions or make loans upon terms that to the ignorant will have a watery, if not a usurious aspect.

Easy chair economists may disapprove of it, but it is a sounder policy for a railroad to borrow money at 3 per cent. and issue an equivalent amount of stock as a bonus to obtain the loan, than to sell a 6 per cent. bond for the same amount. The funds realized are the same, but in the former case the fixed charge is less and the stock affords an incentive to its holders to employ the ability, energy and industry necessary to the financial success of the property. Such water is as necessary to the building of a new railroad or the healthy development of an old one as blood, which is more than nine parts water, is to the human body.

III
HISTORY OF AMERICAN RAILWAYS

"The inventor of the railroad ought to be ranked among the chief builders of the American Union."—John Fiske.

If there are canals all over the face of the planet Mars it must be because there are no railways in Mars. But for the inspiration of James Watt and the genius of George Stephenson we might still be as dependent on canals for artificial waterways as were the almost human beavers before Venice was mistress of the seas and the internal transportation of Holland was the envy of less favored nations.

It is impossible for the present generation to realize what it owes to the railways, which, with their bands of steel, fairly bind the United States in an indissoluble union, without a glance back at the conditions prevailing on this continent before their introduction. Between the first English settlement of Virginia, whose tercentennial we are now celebrating, and the building of the first real railway from Baltimore to Ellicott's, not a step forward had been taken to expedite communication any considerable distance away from tidewater and navigable rivers. The first practical steamboat had made its appearance on the Clyde in 1802. Five years later it took Robert Fulton's Clermont 32 hours to make the trip from New York to Albany—an average speed of less than 5 miles an hour.

In 1818 the first steamboat crossed the Atlantic in 26 days —a feat which has been accomplished by sailing vessels in practically half the time.

In the matter of land transportation the world in the centuries between had not improved upon the road making of the Romans. No advance had been made on the motive power of the horse, the sure-footed pack mule and the hump-backed "ship of the desert." At the opening of the 19th century, as now, the United States, standing in greater need of internal means of transportation than any other country on earth, had the poorest public roads of any civilized community.

That we may fully appreciate the physical conditions in the

republic before the railways came to bind it into a physical as well as a political union of sovereign states, let me present them as described in a few salient paragraphs culled almost at random from Henry Adams' "American History During the First Administration of Thomas Jefferson." No running comment is necessary to suggest the contrast:

"According to the census of 1800 the United States of America contained 5,308,483 persons"—one-fifth of them negro slaves.

"Even after two centuries of struggle the land was still untamed.

"The center of population rested within eighteen miles of Baltimore.

"Except in political arrangement, the interior was little more civilized than in 1750 and was not much easier to penetrate than when LaSalle and Hennepin found their way to the Mississippi more than a century before.

"A great exception broke this rule. Two wagon roads crossed the Alleghany Mountains in Pennsylvania; while a third passed through Virginia southwestward to the Holston River and Knoxville in Tennessee.

"Nowhere did eastern settlements touch the western. At least one hundred miles of mountainous country held the two regions everywhere apart. The shore of Lake Erie, where alone contact seemed easy, was still unsettled.

"The same bad roads and difficult rivers, connecting the same small towns, stretched into the same forests in 1800 as when the armies of Braddock and Amherst pierced the western and northern wilderness.

"Even by water, along the seaboard, communication was as slow and almost as irregular as in colonial days. The voyage to Europe was comparatively more comfortable and more regular than the voyage from New York to Albany.

"If America was to be developed along the lines of water communication alone, by such means as were known to Europe, Nature had decided that the experiment of a single republican government must meet with extreme difficulties. By water an Erie Canal was already foreseen; by land, centuries of labor could alone conquer those obstacles which Nature per mitted to be overcome. Highways furnished no sure measure of progress. No matter how good the road, it could not compete with water, nor could heavy freights in great quantities be hauled long distances without extravagant cost.

"At any known rate of travel Nashville could not be reached in less than a fortnight or three weeks from Philadelphia.

"Politically each group of States lived a life apart.

"In the Northern States, four miles an hour was the average speed for any coach between Bangor and Baltimore. Beyond the Potomac the roads became steadily worse, until south of Petersburg even the mails were carried on horseback.

"Of eight rivers between Monticello and Washington, Jefferson wrote, 'five have neither bridges nor boats.'

"The usual charge (for passengers) in the Northern States was **six cents a mile** by stage.

"The Saxon farmer of the eighth century enjoyed most of the comforts known to Saxon farmers of the eighteenth.

"Fifty or a hundred miles inland more than half the homes were log cabins, which might or might not enjoy the luxury of a glass window."*

"As a rule American capital was absorbed in shipping or agriculture, whence it could not suddenly be withdrawn. No stock exchange existed, and no broker exclusively engaged in stock-jobbing, for there were few stocks.

"A probable valuation of the whole United States in 1800 was $1,800,000,000, equal to $328 for each human being, including slaves; or $418 to each free white.

"Taxes amounted to little or nothing, and wages averaged about a dollar a day."

Such, in brief, is Mr. Adams' description of the conditions prevailing in the United States at the beginning of the nineteenth century. That they had been but little bettered prior to the advent of railways is the testimony of other historians, from De Tocqueville down. The observant philosophic French-

(*) In passing it may be noted that in 1809 Abraham Lincoln was born in one of these log cabins without the luxury of a glass window.

man whose "Democracy in America" was published in 1835, found that,

"The valley of the Mississippi is, upon the whole, the most magnificent dwelling place prepared by God for man's abode; and yet it may be said that at present it is but a mighty desert."

Daniel Webster, with oratorical license, ridiculed the possibility of the present State of Washington becoming a part of the Union, on the ground that a Senator elected from that State could not reach the national capital before the expiration of his term of office. Today Senator Foster can reach Washington from Tacoma in half the time it took Webster to get to Washington when first elected to the Senate from Massachusetts.

From the dawn of civilization canals had been the means by which man had sought to supplement Nature's waterways in the transportation of merchandise, especially of a bulky or heavy nature. There were canals in Egypt seventeen centuries before Christ, and a canal mania raged in England seventeen centuries after that central event in the upward progress of mankind.

The first canal opened in the United States was that connecting Boston with Concord river in 1804. But the active period of canal digging did not come until later when, in 1825, the Erie Canal was opened from Albany to Buffalo. This was the cause of universal rejoicing throughout the country. Begun in 1817, eight years and between eight and nine million dollars were spent in its completion. Although it was 352 miles long and 40 feet wide at the top, it was so shallow—only 4 feet —that it was irreverently spoken of as the longest and most expensive gutter in the world.

The joyful tidings of its official opening was boomed to New York by relays of cannons in 80 minutes—which was transmitting the news with an approach to lightning rapidity for those days.

By means of this marvel of early American energy three fast-walking horses were enabled to draw a canal boat four miles an hour, and we read that "At the end of the fourth day from Schenectady the jaded traveller reached Buffalo." But more important was the fact that, where previous to the building of the canal "it cost $5 and 30 days to ship 100 pounds from Philadelphia to Columbus, Ohio, after it opened the time was reduced to 20 days and the cost to $2.50!" In every way it answered the expectations of its enthusiastic projectors, whose enterprise was repaid by seeing its business double during the first seven years.

In 1835 the Erie canal, at a cost of $25,000,000, was enlarged to 70 feet wide at the top and 40 at the bottom. It had been deepened to 7 feet and provided with 72 locks. This raised its aggregate cost to about $34,000,000, or $97,000 per mile, an expenditure fully justified by the results. By 1852 its receipts reached $3,000,000 a year, or nearly three times what they were in 1826. In the meantime its tolls had been reduced to one-third the original charges. Then began its struggle with railway competition, lasting until 1871, when it finally failed to pay expenses of maintenance. In spite of this demonstration of the impotence of canals to cope with railways, the legislature of New York has not hesitated to renew the contest by expending $100,000,000 for the enlargement and improvement of the old waterway.

Judge Cooley has summed up the result of the struggle between waterways and railways in the memorable words: "The experience of the country has demonstrated that the artificial waterways can not be successful competitors with the railroads on equal terms."

Just as the American people, with characteristic energy, were projecting canals in every direction, George Stephenson succeeded in demonstrating the feasibility of substituting steam for horses in the propulsion of cars on rails. When he combined the escape-steam blast, which provided the draft necessary for a hot fire, and the tubular boiler to multiply the heating surface, the knell of canals on this continent was struck, although many years were to elapse before it was realized.

In 1825, the same memorable year that saw the opening of the Erie Canal, the Stockton and Darlington railway was opened for passengers, and in 1829 Stephenson's locomotive, the "Rocket," attained a speed of 29½ miles an hour. It was this feat of speed that hastened the struggle with the slow-going canal boat, and no thought as to the locomotive's efficiency in drawing heavy loads—something not dreamed of in the minds of engineers experimenting with engines weighing from 3 to 7 tons—the lighter machines having the preference for American roads. The impossibility of canals responding to the American passion for speed finally sealed their fate, outside the deliberations of political conventions and legislative bodies.

The United States is most truly a land of "magnificent distances." Before the era of railways its inhabitants were almost as isolated, so far as means of rapid communication were concerned, as were the different tribes which roamed the continent before the voyage of Columbus. The horse or mule power canal boat was "slow freight" compared with the swift moccasin shod despatch bearer of Pontiac. The almost magical transformation that came across the physical possibilities of the United States with the introduction of the steam locomotive has given to the genesis of the American railway an increasing fascination for American historians. To them the fact that the first tram-road was built from the granite quarries at Quincy, Mass., to Neponset river in 1826 to transport stones for the construction of Bunker Hill monument obscures the fact that it was not a railway in any true sense, being merely a quarry road operated by gravity and horse power. It was not even the first of its kind in the United States and never rose to the dignity of a railway until purchased by the Old Colony Railroad Company in 1872. Then for the first time its relaid T rails felt the swift triumphant tread of locomotive wheels.

Another gravity road frequently mentioned in the early histories of American railways was built at Mauch Chunk, Pennsylvania, in 1827, and still another for the Carbondale and Honesdale Railroad the following year. It was on the last named road that the first locomotive used in the United States, the "Stourbridge Lion," built in England, had its trial trip. Although its weight is stated as only 6 or 7 tons, it was found too heavy for the primitive tracks of those days.

To the Baltimore and Ohio belongs the credit of being the first American railway designed and built for both passenger and freight traffic. At the ceremony of breaking ground for this road on July 4, 1828, Charles Carroll of Carrollton, then in his 92d year, said, "I consider this among the most important acts of my life, second only to that of signing the Declaration of Independence, if even second to that." He lived to see it completed to the Point of Rocks, 73 miles from Baltimore. Originally operated as a horse railroad, the Baltimore and Ohio was the scene of the celebrated contest between a horse drawn car

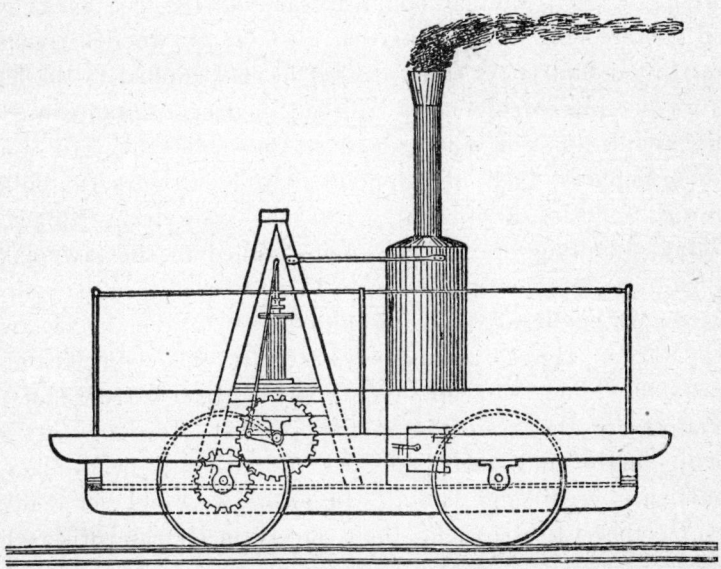

PETER COOPER'S LOCOMOTIVE, 1830.

and the experimental locomotive, Tom Thumb, built by Peter Cooper. Unfortunately for the engine, the belt that worked Mr. Cooper's contrivance for blowing the fire slipped off the drum at a critical stage of the race, and before it could be readjusted the "gallant gray" of the story came in an easy winner. But even in this contest the "iron horse" demonstrated its superiority, barring accidents, over the horse which for ages had been the recognized symbol of power and speed. The Baltimore and Ohio road was opened for traffic for 14 miles in 1830— the year Abraham Lincoln left his mother's log cabin to shift for himself. Within the past eight years the original main line between Relay, 9 miles from Baltimore, and Washington Junction has been entirely reconstructed, including the straightening of curves and a reduction of grades, at a cost of over $3,000,000, or $52,000 per mile.

To Colonel John Stevens of Hoboken seems to be due the high honor of being the first conspicuous American persistently to urge the construction of locomotives on railways for long distance transportation on this continent. He built and ran a steamboat nine years before Fulton built the Clermont, and also patented a multi-tubular boiler as early as 1803. Stevens built and operated the first engine that ever ran on wooden tracks in the United States. As early as 1811 he had applied to the legislature of New Jersey for a railroad charter. Disappointed in this application, he endeavored to persuade the Erie Canal Commissioners, then just appointed in New York, to build a railroad instead of a canal across the state from Albany to Buffalo. Failing of this, he again applied to the law makers of his own state, and this time, in 1815, secured the first railroad charter in the New World, to build a road to join the Delaware and Raritan rivers, connecting at either end with steamboat lines for Philadelphia and New York. His road did not materialize, for the same reason that for yet a dozen years was to nip in the bud many similarly promising projects—lack of confidence, credit and capital. Investors were not yet ready to assume the risk of placing their money in an enterprise where the investment was certain and irrevocable but the profits were still problematical. In those days the necessary funds had to be secured by selling securities at a discount.

Turned down by New York and having made a "dry haul" in New Jersey, Colonel Stevens next directed his attention to Philadelphia, where, through the aid of some of its business men, in 1823 he secured a charter to build a railroad from Philadelphia to Columbia, a town on the Susquehanna twenty-seven miles south of Harrisburg. Some of the privileges granted in this charter, says MacMasters, seem curious enough. "The charter was to be in force for ten years; the rails were to cross all pikes and roads on causeways and the company might charge seven cents a ton per mile on freight moving westward, and half that sum on freight bound east."

Although this charter was subsequently repealed and the State of Pennsylvania itself assumed the task of building a railroad from Philadelphia through Lancaster to Columbia, the charter to Stevens, with its provisions for a seven cent rate per ton mile, is worth recalling for the contrast it affords with the rate of the Pennsylvania Railroad Company of 59/100 of a cent in 1906. Before 1830 the potentialities that lay behind railroads were fully recognized, but the means to grasp the opportunity, namely—money and labor, were scarce and almost impossible to get.

Rich as the histories of those early days are in stories and incidents showing with what persevering enthusiasm and ingenuity that generation of Americans approached the task of adopting and adapting the railway to the needs and conditions of the country, they are singularly shy of accurate data as to the cost of construction. Somewhere it is told that the four miles of the Quincy tramway cost "about $34.000" or $8,500 per mile. With nice exactness we know that the first powerful 7-ton Stephenson locomotive brought to this country "cost $4,869.59, including freight, duties and insurance." We know that the first railways consisted of local lines built generally to connect waterways, that they sought level routes, that they avoided steep grades; that Colonel Stevens had to build a circular railway to demonstrate that a locomotive could haul a train around curves; that the first rails were long wooden stringers protected on the top from the wear of the wheels by strap iron nailed on, and that the locomotives only weighed a few tons and gave more promise of speed than of tractive power. Engineers still doubted the adhesion of a smooth wheel on a smooth rail. There were no through routes in 1830, the longest road actually under construction being from Charleston 135 miles to Hamburg, South Carolina.

We know that the country highway of those days cost from $300 to $500 to build and the rate to move a ton mile on it was about 25 cents.

We know that the early turnpikes cost from $3,000 to $5,000 and reduced the cost of moving a ton to 20 cents a mile, at which figure the average rate stands today. According to a recent bulletin of the Bureau of Statistics the present team haul cost to agriculture averages 23 cents per ton mile, the average on wheat, corn and oats being 19 cents, fruit and vegetables from 28 to 31, and on cotton 27 cents per ton mile.

But we do not know whether the first railways cost more or less than the $25,000 a mile of the original Erie four foot gutter. All we do know of them in this respect is that the opportunity for them was as broad as the continent, the necessity for them apparent, the demand for them insistent and imperative, while the money with which they were financed had to be borrowed mostly in England and Europe at 8 to 10%, and everything that went into their construction had to be brought from abroad or built at home in primitive fashion. The inevitable discount on the sale of securities was the "water" without which American railways could not have been built.

The final picture of the condition of the United States before the railways came to bind its isolated communities into one homogeneous nation is afforded by the National census of that year:

United States Census, 1830.

Alabama	309,527	Missouri	140,455
Arkansas	30,388	New Hampshire	269,328
Connecticut	297,675	New Jersey	320,823
Delaware	76,748	New York	1,918,608
Florida	34,730	North Carolina	737,987
Georgia	516,823	Ohio	937,903
Illinois	157,445	Pennsylvania	1,348,233
Indiana	343,031	Rhode Island	97,199
Kentucky	687,917	S. Carolina	581,185
Louisiana	215,739	Tennessee	681,904
Maine	399,455	Vermont	280,652
Maryland	447,040	Virginia	1,211,405
Massachusetts	610,408	District of Columbia	39,834
Michigan	31,639	U. S. Sailors and persons stationed abroad	5,318
Mississippi	136,621		
		Total	12,866,020

The omissions of this table are its most significant features. Where are the great states of California, Colorado, Idaho, Iowa,

Kansas, Minnesota, Montana, Nebraska, Nevada, the Dakotas, Oregon, Texas, Utah, Washington, Wisconsin, Wyoming, Oklahoma and the territories? They were waiting for the railways; and most of them had to wait three decades longer before they knew the real rush of settlers which came when the railways, with admirable boldness, ventured to build into the wilderness, in many instances before the Indians had finally left it.

Before closing this brief story of the beginnings of American railways, it may be permitted to pass in review their first steps toward the conquest of the continent.

As its name implies, the Baltimore and Ohio was chartered to build a railway from the city of Baltimore to the Ohio river, a distance of over 300 miles. It did not reach its destination until 1853. Only half the distance, with a branch to Washington, was completed within the first decade.

DE WITT CLINTON ENGINE AND TRAIN,
AT THE OPENING OF THE MOHAWK AND HUDSON RAILROAD SEPTEMBER, 1831.

When the State of Pennsylvania took the construction of the Philadelphia and Columbia railway off the hands of Colonel Stevens' company, the line was located in 1828 and construction commenced in the year following. This was the first railway work undertaken by a State government. About twenty miles at the eastern end was opened for travel in 1832 and by 1834 the entire line, with two tracks, was completed. Both passenger and freight cars were owned by individuals or companies, who furnished the horses or mules to haul them, paying the State toll for the use of the road. At first the State owned two locomotives and the number was increased so that by 1834 animal power on the long stretches of the road was discontinued. A regular toll was charged by the State for the use of its locomotives.

McMasters' description of the trip west over this early state road gives a vivid summary of the hybrid railroad and canal travel in the early thirties.

"It was then the custom," says the historian, "for travelers going west from Philadelphia to leave their names and addresses with the agent of some transportation line the day before departure, in order that the "bus" which went the rounds of the city early every morning should call for and carry them and their baggage to the depot. Once there the passengers were hurried into the cars which were coupled in pairs, their luggage was piled on the roofs, and the little trains were hauled by horses to the foot of an inclined plane on the west bank of the Schuylkill River near Belmont. Up this plane they were pulled by

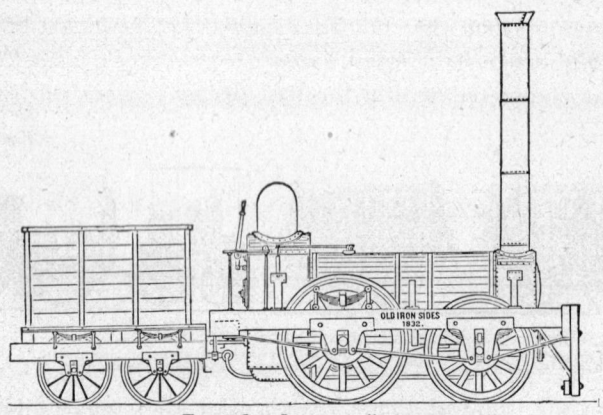

THE "OLD IRONSIDES," 1832
BALDWIN'S FIRST LOCOMOTIVE. WEIGHT 5 TONS.

a stationary engine and rope, and when all were at the top the train of ten or a dozen cars was attached to a little puffing, wheezing locomotive without a cab, without a brake, and whose tall stack sent forth volumes of smoke mingled with red-hot cinders. But this was nothing to what happened when the train, rolling along at a rate of nine miles an hour, crossed a bridge. In those days the floors and trusses of such structures were protected by roofing them over and boarding up the sides almost to the eaves. To raise the roof so high above the rail that the tall stack of the locomotive might pass under would have been costly. The stacks therefore were jointed, and when crossing a bridge the upper half was dropped down and the whole train was enveloped in a cloud of smoke and live cinders.

"A ride of five or more hours, according as the rails were dry or wet, brought the travelers to Lancaster, where they spent the night, and at four the next morning were up and ready to go on. No necessity existed for so early a start, for the distance from Lancaster to Columbia was but twelve miles and the travelers could not leave Columbia till four in the afternoon. But as they had been fed and sheltered at the hotel at Lancaster, it seemed fair that the Red Lion at Columbia should have them at breakfast and dinner.

"At Columbia the railroad ended and the canal began, and there, every week day about four in the afternoon, a few blasts on a horn gave warning that the packet was ready to start. The canal wound along the east bank of the Susquehanna to a point opposite the mouth of the Juniata, crossed by a viaduct to the west shore, and went up the valley of the Juniata through most beautiful scenery to Hollidaysburg at the foot of the Alleghany Mountains. There canal navigation ended. There the traveler spent the night of the second day after leaving Lancaster and early next morning began a journey which none but the boldest

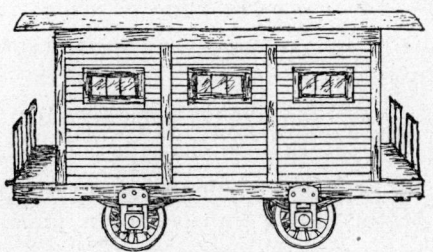

PASSENGER COACH USED ON THE PORTAGE RAILROAD OVER THE ALLEGHANY MOUNTAINS IN 1835.

ventured to take over the portage railroad. The cars were drawn by horses from Hollidaysburg some four miles to the foot of inclined plane No. 10. An endless rope passed up the middle of the right-hand track, around a series of great drums at the top, down the left-hand track and around other drums to the foot of the right-hand track. Made fast to this rope, the cars, two at a time, were pulled up the incline to level No. 10. Along this they were drawn by horses to the foot of incline No. 9, and by repetitions of these processes to the summit of level No. 6, which crossed the crest of the mountain.

"The traveler was then fourteen hundred feet above the canal at Hollidaysburg, and was about to be lowered eleven hundred and seventy-one feet by another series of inclined planes and levels to the basin of the Western Canal at Johnstown. Level No. 2 was fourteen miles long, passed through wild and beautiful mountain scenery and the longest tunnel in the country. Another incline and another level, four miles long, brought the traveler to Johnstown. There a change was made from railroad cars to a canal packet boat, which passed down the valleys of the Kiskiminetas and the Alleghany to Pittsburg."

This description of a journey which consumed five days where the Pennsylvania covers the same distance in seven hours, fairly represents the contrast between travel only 70 years ago and today. In 1851 the State commenced the construction of another line to avoid the ten inclined planes across the Alleghanies, but in 1857 before the work was completed sold both the old and the new portages and the canal sections to the Pennsylvania Railroad Company, which had previously built its own line across the mountains. In 1858 the State disposed of its remaining canals and abandoned its system of transportation. But who will say that all that the State of Pennsylvania paid and sank in its experiments with government ownership and operation of this great transportation undertaking is not properly to be reckoned as a part, and a very essential part, of the cost of construction of American railways. The fact that the road and canal were sold for a song compared with their cost, and that scarcely a vestige of the State venture, except right of way, remains of service to the public today does not wipe out the obligation of the original investment. Besides, the people of the United States in our day are millions richer for the pioneer work of the State which a great railway company subsequently had to reconstruct or abandon to perfect its magnificent service across the Alleghanies.

How subsequently the railroads pushed their way westward until they reached the Pacific is thus summarized in a paragraph from Poor's Manual for 1870-71.

"In 1851 the Erie Railroad was opened from the Hudson to Lake Erie—an event of first rate importance in the history of our railroad enterprises. In the following year the completion of the Michigan Central and Michigan Southern lines carried the railroad system of the country as far west as Chicago.*

THE RECONSTRUCTED "PIONEER" OF THE CHICAGO & NORTHWESTERN. THIS 10 TON LOCOMOTIVE REACHED CHICAGO BY SCHOONER OCT. 10, 1848.

In 1854, this system was carried to the Mississippi River by the completion of the Chicago and Rock Island Railroad. In 1853, The Baltimore and Ohio Railroad was completed to the Ohio River, at Wheeling. In 1854, the Pennsylvania Railroad was completed to Pittsburg. In 1856, the Illinois Central Railroad was completed from Chicago to the Mississippi River, at Cairo. The Chicago, Burlington and Quincy Railroad was opened to Quincy in 1856. The Pittsburg, Fort Wayne and Chicago, extending the Pennsylvania Railroad to Chicago, was completed in 1858. In 1859, the Hannibal and St. Joseph Railroad was extended from the Mississippi to the Missouri. In 1866, the Cedar Rapids and Missouri was completed to the Missouri River opposite Omaha. In 1867, a line of railroad was formed between Chicago and St. Paul, Minnesota; and in 1869, by the completion of the Pacific Railroad—the greatest enterprise of the kind ever yet achieved—a continuous line of railway was formed from the Atlantic to the Pacific Ocean, a distance of nearly 3,500 miles."

---

*Lake Michigan and not Chicago was the original objective of these roads.

In concluding his review of the thirty years of railway achievement in America prior to 1870, the editor of Poor's Manual in that year said: "The early roads, as already remarked, were neither designed nor adapted to serve the purpose of commerce so much as of travel. The frail works first constructed were by no means adequate to a heavy merchandise traffic. They were constructed with longitudinal sills covered with thin flat bars of iron. With such structures, neither high speed nor heavy trains were possible."

And yet the early roads were as adequate to the traffic of 1870 as the roads and equipment of 1870 would be to the traffic of 1907. The "early roads" revolutionized the transportation system of the United States; they made its remote places assessible; they brought millions upon millions of acres of wilderness, prairie and forest within the radius of man's dominion; they enabled the union of the states to expand from ocean to ocean; they brought the American farm and factory within trading distance of foreign markets; but without another revolution, in which they have been reconstructed from Portland to San Diego, the railways of 1870 would no more have been able to handle the traffic of 1907, they have been chiefly instrumental in creating, than would Peter Cooper's "Tom Thumb" have been equal to hauling a passenger train of 1876 from San Francisco to the Centennial at Philadelphia.

Wooden bridges, strap rails and dirt or gravel ballast sufficed for the earlier traffic of American railways. Before 1870 these had given place to iron bridges, 56 lb. iron T rails and some broken stone ballast as traffic expanded. And these in turn have been superseded by steel or masonry structures, 70 to 100 lb. steel rails and more carefully prepared road beds to meet modern demands.

In 1835 it would have taken something more than human prescience to have foreseen such a growth as is shown in the following table of way freight on the Camden and Amboy railroad, 1835-1869:

Way Freight on the Camden and Amboy 1835 to 1869.

Year.	Tons Carried.	Year.	Tons Carried.
1835	1,451	1855	71,764
1840	3,356	1860	83,543
1845	7,480	1865	182,541
1850	20,515	1869	429,029

In 1906 the United Railroads of New Jersey division of the Pennsylvania Railroad, into which the Camden and Amboy was merged, carried a total of 30,732,210 tons.

The miracle of such revolutions in ability to handle traffic, common throughout the country, is that it has been accomplished without material increase, if any, to the net capitalization of American railways per mile. Millions of dollars were expended to bring the original roads up to the requirements of 1870, and other millions have been spent to bring the roads of 1870 up to the standard and performance of today, while the net capitalization stands at $54,421 per mile against a gross of $59,726 in 1870, when intercorporate holdings were comparatively insignificant.

With 1870 the historical review of American railways ends, and the period of comprehensive statistics begins. This may be prefaced with a table showing the mileage of American railways by states in successive decades:

MILEAGE OF RAILWAYS IN THE UNITED STATES BY STATES SINCE 1841.

	1841.	1850.	1860.	1870.	1880.	1890.	1900.	1905.
Alabama	46	183	743	1,157	1,843	3,147	4,219	4,776
Arkansas	....	....	38	256	859	2,112	3,341	4,183
California	....	....	23	925	2,195	4,147	5,744	6,477
Colorado	....	....	....	157	1,570	4,154	4,587	5,027
Connecticut	102	402	601	742	923	1,007	1,023	1,018
Delaware	39	39	127	197	275	322	346	335
Florida	....	21	402	446	518	2,389	3,272	3,590
Georgia	271	643	1,420	1,845	2,459	4,105	5,639	6,442
Idaho	....	....	....	....	206	941	1,261	1,465
Illinois	22	111	2,790	4,823	7,851	9,843	10,997	11,830
Indiana	....	228	2,163	3,177	4,373	5,891	6,469	6,915
Iowa	....	....	655	2,683	5,400	8,347	9,180	9,871
Kansas	....	....	....	1,501	3,400	8,806	8,719	8,841
Kentucky	28	78	534	1,017	1,530	2,694	3,059	3,286
Louisiana	40	80	335	450	652	1,657	2,824	4,011
Maine	11	245	472	786	1,005	1,312	1,915	2,028
Maryland	*259	*259	*386	*671	*1,040	1,138	1,376	1,434
Massachusetts	373	1,035	1,264	1,480	1,915	2,093	2,118	2,119
Michigan	138	342	779	1,638	3,938	6,788	8,193	8,789
Minnesota	....	....	....	1,092	3,151	5,466	6,942	7,992
Mississippi	14	75	862	990	1,127	2,292	2,919	3,672
Missouri	....	....	817	2,000	3,965	5,897	6,867	8,039
Montana	....	....	....	....	106	2,181	3,010	3,309
Nebraska	....	....	....	705	1,953	5,274	5,684	5,833
Nevada	....	....	....	593	739	924	909	1,180
New Hampshire	53	467	661	736	1,015	1,133	1,239	1,267
New Jersey	186	206	560	1,125	1,684	2,034	2,237	2,224
New York	538	1,361	2,682	3,928	5,957	7,462	8,121	8,336
North Carolina	87	283	937	1,178	1,486	2,904	3,808	4,210
North Dakota	....	....	....	†65	†1,225	1,940	2,731	3,233
Ohio	36	575	2,946	3,538	5,792	7,719	8,774	9,259
Oregon	....	....	....	159	508	1,268	1,723	1,813
Pennsylvania	754	1,240	2,598	4,656	6,191	8,307	10,277	11,043
Rhode Island	50	68	108	136	210	205	211	212
South Carolina	204	289	973	1,139	1,427	2,095	2,794	3,160
South Dakota	....	....	....	....	....	2,485	2,849	3,067
Tennessee	....	....	1,253	1,492	1,843	2,709	3,124	3,561
Texas	....	....	307	711	3,244	7,911	9,873	11,983
Utah	....	....	....	257	842	1,090	1,447	1,774
Vermont	....	290	554	614	914	913	1,012	1,058
Virginia	223	384	1,379	1,486	1,893	3,142	3,729	3,950
Washington	....	....	....	....	289	1,698	2,890	3,367
West Virginia	61	97	352	387	691	1,305	2,198	2,929
Wisconsin	....	20	905	1,525	3,155	5,468	6,496	7,211
Wyoming	....	....	....	459	512	941	1,228	1,247
Arizona	....	....	....	....	349	1,061	1,411	1,665
District of Columbia	....	....	....	....	....	30	31	32
Indian Territory	....	....	....	....	‡289	1,046	1,322	2,638
New Mexico	....	....	....	....	758	1,284	1,752	2,534
Oklahoma	....	....	....	....	....	167	827	2,625
United States	6,535	9,021	30,626	52,922	93,267	159,271	192,940	217,017

United States, 1906 222,340

*Includes District of Columbia.
†Includes South Dakota.
‡Includes Oklahoma.

IV

PRESENT CAPITALIZATION

	Amount.	Per Mile of Line.
Gross capital (including duplications), 1906	$14,570,421,478	$67,936
Net capital (excluding duplications), 1906	11,671,940,649	54,421
Net capital per mile of track		37,746

Nearly all discussions of railway problems have been confused and the value of their conclusions vitiated by fixing popular attention on the gross figures of capitalization, income and profits. To what extent this is calculated to mislead the unwary and deceive the uninformed, may be judged by the foregoing table.

From the date of his first annual report on the "Statistics of Railways of the United States" (March 1, 1889) down to his latest report (August 20, 1906), Henry C. Adams, Statistician of the Interstate Commerce Commission, has shown the liveliest interest in this question of railway capitalization. Reference has already been made to his early views on the imperative necessity for an estimate of the cost and value of the railways, to be made "by competent authority, free from outside influences and clothed with ample power for the investigation." Coincident with this expression of his views in regard to cost, in his first report he discussed the amount and character of capital invested in the railway industry, applying the term "railway capital" to all forms of property "that draws its revenues from railway operations." This he found to consist of stock, all forms of funded debt for the security of which railway plant or railway income is mortgaged, and the floating capital necessary to keep fixed investments in a profitable state of activity.

Following out his idea that this capital should include the property that drew its "revenues from railway operations," Mr. Adams' first tables included under the term capital all "stocks, bonds, car trust obligations, receivers' certificates and current liabilities." In his explanation of his course in including current liabilities in his classification, he said: "Stocks and bonds make up fixed investments. They represent fixed capital. But fixed capital cannot be a source of profit except through the constant application of circulating capital." This circulating capital, he concluded, was fairly represented in "current liabilities," which were included in the official capitalization tables until 1896, when, at the request of the Association of American Railway Accounting Officers, they were excluded from the capital account.

As early as 1867 "Poor's Manual of the Railroads of the United States" had attempted to give the capitalization of American railways, then estimated to be $1,172,881,000 or about $40,000 per mile. That this was little more than a conscientious guess was quickly demonstrated, when, in the fifth issue of that valuable work, for the first time anything like a comprehensive summary of the affairs of American railways was made accessible to the public. Even this was not as exhaustive as the publishers of the Manual hoped to make it, for in the sixth series they apologized for the "meagre and incomplete" reports from some of the companies, and only vouched "for the correctness of our (its) own statements as far as they go."

In the following table of "Gross Capitalization" compiled from Poor's Manual down to 1888 and the official Statistics of Railways since then, "floating debt" is included prior to 1875 and excluded thereafter. The figures of mileage prior to those for June 30, 1890, include road operated under trackage rights, which were excluded by Mr. Adams in the summaries after that year. This accounts for the increase in capital per mile shown in the official figures between 1889 and 1890. This table is presented for comparative purposes only, and not as properly representing the true situation at any period. Its defects, however, except as to the variations noted, are common to all years. The returns from the Manual are by calendar years, those from the official Statistics by fiscal years:

GROSS CAPITALIZATION.

(Including Stock, Bonds, Income Bonds, Equipment, Trust and Miscellaneous Obligations.)

Year	Miles of Line.	Total Capital.	Capital per Mile of Line.
1871	44,014	$2,004,027,045	$59,720
1872	57,523	3,159,423,057	55,116
1873	66,237	3,784,543,034	57,134
1874	69,273	4,221,763,594	60,425
1875	71,759	4,415,631,630	61,533
1876	73,508	4,468,591,935	60,790
1877	74,112	4,568,597,248	61,644
1878	78,960	4,590,048,793	58,131
1879	79,009	4,715,136,465	59,677
1880	82,146	5,239,548,318	63,783
1881	92,971	6,055,798,785	65,136
1882	104,938	6,692,998,547	63,780
1883	110,381	7,155,205,297	64,768
1884	115,671	7,373,967,813	63,749
1885	123,280	7,518,864,803	60,990
1886	125,144	7,810,125,828	62,409
1887	136,986	8,302,586,330	60,609
1888 (a)	145,333	8,977,758,747	61,704
1888 (b)	136,883	7,733,684,420	56,498
1889	153,385	8,574,046,742	55,892
1890	156,404	8,984,234,616	58,659
1891	161,275	9,290,915,439	59,006
1892	162,275	9,686,146,813	61,130
1893	169,779	9,894,625,239	59,729
1894	175,690	10,190,658,678	59,419
1895	177,746	10,346,754,229	59,650
1896	181,982	10,566,865,771	59,610
1897	183,284	10,635,008,074	59,620
1898	184,648	10,818,554,031	60,343
1899	187,534	11,033,954,898	60,556
1900	192,556	11,491,034,960	61,490
1901	195,561	11,688,147,091	61,531
1902	200,154	12,134,182,964	62,301
1903	205,313	12,599,990,258	63,186
1904	212,243	13,213,124,679	64,265
1905	216,973	13,805,258,121	65,926
1906	222,340	14,570,421,478	67,936
Increase per mile in 35 years			8,210
Increase per mile in 16 years (official)			9,277

(a) Calendar year, Poor's Manual.
(b) Year ending June 30, Interstate Commerce Commission.

It is obvious that if the mileage of track rights deducted from the miles of line to ascertain the capital per mile in the Interstate Commerce Commission reports could have been deducted in the returns from Poor's Manual, the capital per mile would have appeared greater than is shown above for the years down to 1888.

The apparent excess of capital per mile in the returns from Poor's Manual is probably due to an even greater duplication of capital than the later official reports contained.

The apparent decrease in mileage in the official report for 1888 was probably due to the incompleteness of the first reports to the Commission, as the increase in the succeeding year is not warranted by the new construction.

Although valuable as showing the comparative trend of railway capitalization, owing to two errors—one of omission and the other of inclusion—this table fails to afford a truthful statement of the capital situation of the railways at any time during the 36 years it covers. Neither in 1871 nor in 1906 does it show all the trackage on account of which railway capital has been expended, while during the whole period the capital is unduly swelled by including capital invested in securities of other railways.

Manifestly the growth and cost of American railways since 1871 is inadequately expressed in the increase of single track mileage, omitting all reference to the simultaneous increase in miles of auxiliary track and sidings, to say nothing of the accompanying reconstruction of every physical feature of original lines. Reserving comment on this last illusive item of cost represented in capitalization, to be discussed in another connection, the capital cost per "mile of track," as distinguished from mile of line, may be studied to advantage.

Returns for "all other tracks" are first given in Poor's Manual for 1872, where they amount to 11,188 miles, or one mile of "other track" to 5.1 miles of line. By 1880 the mileage of "other track" had increased to 21,977 and bore the proportion of one to 3.7 miles of line.

When the official statistician first took cognizance of "other track" in 1889, he found that it consisted of 8,084 miles of second track, 722 miles of third track, 531 miles of fourth track, and 31,715 miles of yard track, sidings and spurs, making 41,052 miles of other track; or a proportion of one to 3.7 miles of line —the same proportion as in 1880,—a rather remarkable, albeit reassuring, coincidence.

By 1895 the total of "other track" officially reported had risen to 55,528 miles, or a proportion of one to 3.2 miles of line; and in 1906 it had increased to 94,743 miles, or a proportion of one to 2.3 miles of line.

In brief, the miles of auxiliary track during the period for which we have information has increased twice as fast as miles of single track, although the latter in the meantime has almost quadrupled.

In the matter of second track alone, 8 per cent. of the line mileage of the United States is double tracked now against only 5 per cent. in 1889—the actual second track mileage having more than doubled.

The significance of these facts is that any increase there may have been in railway capital per mile during the last thirty years is wholly accounted for by the relatively greater increase in "other track" mileage, which has enabled the railways to meet the advancing tide of traffic.

NET CAPITALIZATION.

Thus far we have dealt with gross capitalization and what it has represented. It is now in order to squeeze the duplication out of that gross total. Unfortunately, prior to 1889 the summaries of statistics fail to disclose to what extent railway capitalization was duplicated by intercorporate investments. That it was extensive is proved by the fact that in 1870 the Pennsylvania Railroad owned stocks and bonds of other corporations to the amount of $23,668,220—a sum equal to more than a third of its capital stock and funded obligations. It was not until well along in the nineties that the New York Central became heavily interested in the securities of other companies, of which in 1906 it held $154,411,052.

Since 1889 the Interstate Commerce Commission reports have contained tables showing the amount of such securities owned by all the railways. In that year these amounted to $1,151,972,901, or 13.5 per cent. of the entire outstanding capital. In 1895, this had risen to $1,447,181,534, or 15 per cent. of such capital, and in 1906 to $2,898,480,829, or slightly less than 20 per cent. of such outstanding stocks and bonds, or 19 per cent. of the total capitalization of $14,570,421,478—including income bonds, equipment trust obligations and miscellaneous obligations.

How this capital account actually stands may be seen at a glance in the following table:

CAPITAL ACCOUNT IN 1906.

Gross Capital Stock—	
Common...	$5,403,001,962
Preferred...	1,400,758,131
Funded Debt—	
Bonds..	6,266,770,962
Miscellaneous obligations...........................	973,647,924
Income bonds.......................................	301,523,400
Equipment trust obligations........................	224,719,099
Total Gross Capital........................	$14,570,421,478
From which deduct—	
Stock owned by railway corporations............. $2,257,175,799	
Bonds owned by railway corporations............. 641,305,030	
Total stock and bonds owned.................	2,898,480,829
Net capitalization..........................	$11,671,940,649
Divided by Mileage—	
222,340 miles of line less 7,865 trackage rights equals 214,475 miles.	
Net Capital per Mile.............................	**$54,421**

"Current Liabilities" are excluded from this computation as in 1905, when they amounted to $953,319,866, they were more than offset by $1,014,288,239 "cash and current assets," $149,371,001 "materials and supplies," and $128,588,790 "sinking funds and sundries." (Vide Interstate Commerce Commission's "Statistics of Railways" 1905, page 99.)

Applying this formula to the data since the figures as to trackage rights and securities owned have been available—to wit, 1890—we arrive at the following correct statement of net capitalization of American railways per mile of line:

NET CAPITALIZATION PER MILE OF LINE, 1890-1905.

Year.	Miles of Line Less Trackage Rights.	Net Capitalization.	Capital per Mile.
1890	153,160	$7,577,327,615	$49,473
1891	157,457	8,007,989,723	50,858
1892	158,452	8,294,689,760	52,348
1893	165,659	8,331,603,006	50,293
1894	171,505	8,646,600,008	50,358
1895	173,460	8,899,572,695	51,421
1896	177,264	9,065,518,857	51,141
1897	178,381	9,168,071,898	51,396
1898	179,285	9,297,167,776	51,856
1899	182,212	9,432,041,731	51,215
1900	186,876	9,547,984,611	51,092
1901	189,955	9,482,649,182	49,925
1902	194,767	9,925,664,171	50,961
1903	199,411	10,281,598,305	51,559
1904	205,604	10,711,794,078	52,099
1905	209,405	11,167,105,992	53,328
1906	214,475	11,671,940,649	54,421
Increase per mile in sixteen years			$4,948

Comparing this increase of $4,948 per mile of net capital with the increase of gross capital for the same period, it will be perceived that by applying the simple touchstone of truth, supplied by the official figures, no less than $4,329 per mile of the fictitious water, we hear so much about in railway capitalization, is not and never has been there.

Conclusive as these figures for 1906 are of the present low and reasonable capitalization of American railways, and while they may be compared instructively with similar figures as to capital cost of railways in other countries, they are susceptible of further rectification before they are finally available for comparison with our past capital per mile.

Attention has already been called to the relatively greater increase of second, third, fourth and other track and sidings (of which there was less than 12,000 miles in 1872 and nearly 95,000 miles in 1906) over single track mileage. It is now proposed to show the comparative course of railway capitalization in the United States since 1889 as applied to miles of track **operated**— this term including single track, second, third, fourth, yard track and sidings—it being submitted that all these are properly included in the capital investment, and it being a matter of common knowledge that much of the auxiliary track represents a higher investment per mile than some original single track mileage.

COMPARATIVE SUMMARY OF NET CAPITALIZATION PER MILE OF TRACK OPERATED, INCLUDING SINGLE TRACK, SECOND TRACK, THIRD TRACK, FOURTH TRACK AND YARD TRACK AND SIDINGS, 1889-1906.

Year.	Miles of All Tracks Operated.	Net Capitalization.	Capital per Mile of Track.
1889	191,001	$7,422,073,841	$38,911
1890	208,612	7,577,327,615	36,322
1891	216,149	8,007,989,723	37,048
1892	222,351	8,294,689,760	37,304
1893	230,137	8,331,603,006	35,768
1894	233,533	8,646,600,008	37,025
1895	233,275	8,899,572,695	38,150
1896	239,140	9,065,518,857	37,908
1897	242,013	9,168,071,898	37,882
1898	245,333	9,297,167,776	37,896
1899	250,142	9,432,041,731	37,307
1900	258,784	9,557,984,611	36,934
1901	265,352	9,482,649,182	35,735
1902	274,195	9,925,664,171	36,195
1903	283,821	10,281,598,305	36,225
1904	297,073	10,711,794,078	36,057
1905	306,796	11,167,105,992	36,399
1906	317,083	11,671,940,649	36,810
Increase per mile in sixteen years 1890-1906.			$ 478

In this table the increase of $4,948 in net capitalization per mile of line shown for the fifteen years 1890 to 1906 dwindles to only $478 per mile during the same years, when the increase in auxiliary track is taken into account. Will anyone conversant with the practical operation of railways dissent from the inclusion of auxiliary tracks in the cost of railways at any stage of their development? If he does, let him calculate what the railways of the United States in 1906 would have been had their auxiliary tracks been increased only pro rata, as they did between 1880 and 1889. We have already seen that there was one mile of auxiliary track to every 3.7 miles of line in 1889. Applying this ratio to the single track mileage of 1906 would have provided only 58,641 miles of auxiliary track against a reported mileage of 94,743. The difference, 36,102 miles, involved new construction just as surely as in the building of original lines. At an average of $10,000 per mile this would require a capital expenditure of $361,020,000. This is a very conservative estimate because most of this auxiliary construction has been in the territory with the densest traffic and where cost of yard space near terminals was highest.

An estimate of $361,020,000 disposes of more than one-third the capitalization represented in the increase of $4,948 per mile between 1890 and 1906 in the table of net capitalization.

The remainder is far more than represented in the increase in the relative number, capacity and cost of equipment per mile during the same period. This increase in number is shown in the following statement:

	1889		1906		Increase per 100 Miles
	Number	No. per 100 Miles Operated	Number	No. per 100 Miles Operated	
Locomotives	29,036	18.6	51,672	23.2	4.6
Passenger cars	25,665	16.4	42,262	19.0	2.6
Freight cars	885,688	577.3	1,916,650	861.8	284.5

The increases per 100 miles of line operated shown in the last column of the above table when applied to the mileage of 1906 produce the following statement of the increase in the capital cost of equipment over what it would have been had the ratio to line remained the same as in 1889:

Excess Over the Ratio of 1889.

	Number	Cost each	Capital Cost
Locomotives	10,225	$12,000	$122,700,000
Passenger cars	5,779	6,000	34,674,000
Freight cars	632,443	900	569,189,700
Total			$726,563,700

This sum added to the estimate of the cost of the excess of auxiliary track over the proportionate increase during the period under consideration makes a total of $1,087,583,700 or $5,072 per mile of line, to place against the increase of $4,948 per mile in net capitalization shown above.

While these estimates are not scientifically accurate, they are so obviously reasonable as to afford convincing proof that in recent years there has been an actual and remarkable shrinkage in the capitalization of American railways when compared with the vast sums that have been invested in their extension, renewal, improvement and re-equipment. Furthermore, it should be borne in mind that these estimates, as to the cost of excess of auxiliary track and equipment, have not taken into account the capital outlay for introducing the block signal system on over 50,000 miles, the equipping of virtually the entire service with automatic couplers and train brakes—not 10% of the cars being so equipped prior to 1889—the reduction of grades, straightening of alignment and relaying of thousands of miles

Track Elevation in Chicago by the Chicago and Western Indiana R. R. Looking South From 49th Street.

of old line with heavier rails, more ties per rail and better ballast.

Nor has the elimination of crossings of highways and railways at grade been a matter of insignificant expense to the railways. In Massachusetts, where the commonwealth and the local authorities bear 35% of the cost, the Railroad Commissioners report that this work since 1890 has cost the railways $16,299,664.

Nearly three times this sum has already been spent by the railways of Illinois, without state or local aid, on track elevation in Chicago alone; and similar work laid out will call for a total

TRACK ELEVATION IN CHICAGO BY THE CHICAGO AND WESTERN INDIANA R. R.
LOOKING NORTH FROM 49TH STREET.

expenditure of $75,000,000, an amount equal to the Census valuation of all the railways of South Carolina in 1904, and more than the construction cost of all the railways of the kingdom of Norway.

It has been estimated that it would cost nearly half a billion dollars to do away with the 8,733 grade crossings in New York State alone!

Whether the railways of the United States are worth their net capitalization as of June 30, 1906—$11,671,940,649 or $54,421 per mile of line or $37,746 per mile of track—is an inquiry that we may now approach from several different points of view.

V

FIRST COST OF CONSTRUCTION

From the earliest records, and despite the financial shifts to which the original builders of American railways were forced to raise capital, the fact stands out through all the statistics that their capital and cost of construction were never far apart. In their early history capital invested and cost of construction were often treated as synonymous, although in 1870 it was said that the stocks and bonds issued by all the companies had not probably produced more than seventy-five cents on the dollar. It was recognized then, though often forgotten since, that the account was about evenly balanced by the net earnings, which in the language of Poor's Manual ('70-71) "have been put into construction without any increase of nominal capital. The cost of old lines, of course, constantly increases, but the average for the whole country is kept down by the new lines which are being opened."

In a table of comparative statistics for the year 1875, accompanying the ninth series of Poor's Manual, the total investment per road mile of American railways is given as $62,725, while the "cost of works per road mile" is placed at $58,874. In 1880 the total investment including floating debt was $5,108,241,906 and the "cost of railroad and equipment" was placed at $4,653,-609,297. The Manual for 1886 thus states the liabilities of the companies owning 127,729 miles of line in 1885:

LIABILITIES.		ASSETS.	
Capital stock	$3,817,697,832	Cost R. R. and Equipment	$7,037,627,350
Funded debt	3,765,727,066	Real estate, stocks, bonds and other investments	946,353,859
Unfunded debt	259,108,281	Cash, bills receivable, current accounts, etc	303,853,405
Current debt	231,040,215		
		Total assets	$8,287,834,614
Total liabilities	$8,073,573,394	**Excess Assets over Liabilities**	214,261,220

This statement contains the unmistakable indication of what was susceptible of bookkeeping proof, as soon as the official statistician segregated the items, that the cost of Construction and Equipment of American railways exceeded their net capitalization, as is shown in the following statement of these items since 1890:

COMPARATIVE STATEMENT OF NET CAPITALIZATION AND COST OF CONSTRUCTION AND EQUIPMENT, 1890 TO 1905.

YEAR	Net Capitalization	Per Mile	Cost of Construction and Equipment	Per Mile
1890	$ 7,577,327,615 153,160 miles	$ 49,473	$ 7,755,387,381 (not given)	
1891	8,007,989,723 157,457 miles	50,858	8,738,533,165 (not given)	
1892	8,294,689,760 158,452 miles	52,348	* 8,564,394,830 143,518 miles	$ 59,674
1893	8,331,603,006 165,659 miles	50,293	8,937,545,760 161,258 miles	55,423
1894	8,646,600,008 171,505 miles	50,416	9,073,470,532 164,008 miles	55,317
1895	8,899,572,695 173,460 miles	51,306	9,203,490,619 167,741 miles	54,867
1896	9,065,518,857 177,264 miles	51,029	9,500,327,733 173,860 miles	54,643
1897	9,168,071,898 178,381 miles	51,396	9,709,329,228 174,673 miles	55,585
1898	9,297,167,776 139,285 miles	51,856	9,750,581,424 170,000 miles	57,336
1899	9,432,041,731 182,212 miles	51,764	9,961,840,805 177,638 miles	56,079
1900	9,547,984,611 186,876 miles	51,092	10,263,313,400 181,437 miles	56,511
1901	9,482,649,182 189,955 miles	49,920	10,405,095,085 182,734 miles	56,941
1902	9,925,664,171 194,411 mi es	51,055	10,658,213,376 187,442 miles	56,861
1903	10,281,598,305 199'411 miles	51,545	10,973,494,903 193,823 miles	56,616
1904	10,711,794,078 205,604 miles	52,099	11,511,537,131 198,841 miles	57,893
1905	11,167,105,992 209,405 miles	53,328	11,951,348,949 203,228 miles	58,807
1906	11,671,949,649 214,475 miles	54,421		

*This decrease is explained by transfer of $541,000,000 included in "Cost of Road" in 1891 to "Miscellaneous" item in General balance Sheet for 1892. This is all the information vouchsafed by the Statistician.

Here we have what Mr. Adams calls the "bookkeeping statement" of the cost of constructing American railways, which on its face shows that during the whole period mentioned **the cost of a part has exceeded the net capitalization of the whole.** The figures in small type, giving the mileage for each year respectively, show that this discrepancy in mileage represented ran as high as 14,934 miles in 1892 and 3,404 miles at its low mark in 1896.

In regard to the annual balance sheets of the railways, from which Mr. Adams compiled these figures of cost of construction, it should be said that he was never satisfied that they accurately represented actual expenditures. Different roads used a diversity of methods in accounting. In 1891 he asked, "Is the balance sheet the true interpretation of the standing of a railway company that expends large sums of money on its roadbed, and charges such expenditures to operating expenses?" Of his own general balance sheet that year, however, he said, "It is doubtless more nearly accurate than any similar statement ever published." And yet, as the note to the above table states, it contained a small item of $541,000,000 in cost of construction which was transferred to "Miscellaneous" account in the following year.

These annual balance sheets bear internal evidence to the fact that they consistently understated the cost of the railway property. For instance, in 1895 the item for "cost of equipment" is given at $571,570,946, to which it had risen gradually during the preceding years. By 1898 this item had declined to $526,347,372, although during the meantime there had been an actual increase of 535 locomotives, 483 passenger cars, and 55,613 freight cars which at prevailing prices could not have cost less than $50,000,000. A decrease in cost of equipment as given in the balance sheet in the face of such facts can only be explained by assuming that during the period of receiverships and reorganizations that prevailed from 1894 to 1898, account ceased to be taken, not only of current expenditures for additional equipment, but of the irrevocable expenditures previously made.

The word "Receiver" does not appear in the exhaustive index to the report of the Statistician for the year ending June 30, 1893. The report for the year following notes, "That never in the history of transportation in the United States has such a large percentage of railway mileage been under the control of receiverships as on June 30, 1894." The receivership record for that and the next five years, which had such an apparent bearing on the shrinkage of the cost of equipment, was as follows:

RAILWAYS IN RECEIVER'S HANDS, 1894-1899.

YEAR	Number of Companies	Miles Operated	Capitalization Involved.
1894	192	40,818	$2,500,000,000
1895	169	37,855	2,439,144,503
1896	151	30,475	1,892,331,464
1897	128	18,861	1,131,278,748
1898	94	12,744	661,575,318
1899	71	9,853	585,878,251

Formidable as is the array of wrecks from the depression of 1894, it does not tell the whole distressing story. During the period covered in the above table no less than 308 roads operating 55,620 miles of line and having an aggregate capitalization of over $3,133,000,000 went into receivers' hands. This means that during six years, less than a decade ago, nearly one-third of the mileage and more than one-third of the capitalized investment of American railways had to seek the shelter of the courts to escape the effects of the financial and industrial storm that swept over the country.

In 1900, when the railways may be said to have emerged from the protectorship of the courts, the report of the Statistician credits them with $588,361,029 for "cost of equipment," or only $16,790,083 more than in 1895, although in the meantime there had been an increase of 1,967 locomotives, 1,601 passenger cars, and 178,676 freight cars, representing an outlay of at least $135,000,000, irrespective of the increased cost of more expensive replacements.

From which it is evident that receiverships have had the effect not only of squeezing the water out of railway capitalization but of excluding expenditures for additional equipment from the "bookkeeping cost" of the railways.

INCOMPLETE RECORDS OF COST.

There are as many reasons why it is impracticable to get at the actual cost of the railways of the United States as there are railway companies—and the last official report gives a list of 2,167 of them—to say nothing of those which have become extinct since Carrol of Carrolton turned the first sod for the B. and O. In the beginning they were independent corporations subject to few regulations as common carriers and none as to their methods of accounting. The cost of the Quincy tramway is a mere guess of "about $34,000." The capital subscribed for building the 61 miles of the Camden and Amboy Railroad in 1830 was $4,000,000, or over $65,000 per mile. But this included the digging a canal. The so-called "Mauch Chunk Railroad," a mere 3 ft. 6 in. wooden tramway built in 1827, from Mauch Chunk, 9 miles to the coal mines, cost $3,500 per mile. We know to a cent what the first imported Stephenson locomotive cost, for it had to be declared at the Custom House. We are told that it cost one hundred dollars to transport a ton of freight from Buffalo to Albany before the construction of the Erie Canal, and know approximately that it cost $97,000 per mile to build and improve the great waterway that was to remove the land barrier between the East and West. But we have no authoritative knowledge on which to base a comprehensive guess as to what was the original cost of the instrumentality which, after a generation of competition, was to put the Erie Canal out of business.

Buried in the archives of a thousand and one companies might be found the records of the cost of their original lines had anyone the time, patience and interest necessary for the task. But no scrutiny however conscientious and searching could possibly separate the myriad items of expenditures for improvements and betterments from the current expenses for maintenance of way, structures and equipment during three-quarters of a century of railway expansion.

There was no system about and no supervision above either the beginnings or the bookkeeping of railways in America. They sprang into existence in response to the demand for communication between settlements on the tidewaters and water routes of the country. Canals served well enough to carry heavy or bulky goods, but were tedious for passengers and in the North closed to traffic in winter. The railways came sporadically wherever the conditions promised profit, they were financed with difficulty and frequent disappointments, except during periods of speculative mania, and were often not built by the parties who projected them and paid the initial cost of surveys and location. This kind of costly experience has lasted all through the history of railways at all stages of their initiation, construction, development and survival. The records of their cost have been lost or rendered valueless in the numerous financial crises and combinations and reorganizations that have marked and scarred their history.

Originally capitalized at $5,000,000, by 1843, when 188 miles had been built, the Baltimore and Ohio had cost $7,623,600, or over $40,000 per mile.

The Charleston and Hamburg road of South Carolina, chartered in 1829, for which the first American locomotives placed in actual service were built, is said to have cost only $1,750,000 for 135 miles completed in 1834, but before 1840 it was sold to the Louisville, Cincinnati and Charleston Railroad Company for $2,400,000, or nearly $18,000 per mile. It was an unusually straight and level road, through a gently undulating country, and was cheaply constructed even for those times.

The original cost of the New England roads was much higher; that of the Boston and Lowell, commenced in 1831 and completed in 1835, being $1,505,645 up to November 30, 1836, or $56,600 per mile; that of the Boston and Worcester, commenced in 1831, $1,700,000, or $38,700 per mile—$250,000 being expended for real estate, right of way, depot buildings and machinery; that of the Great Western Railroad (now Boston and Albany west of Worcester) was estimated at $4,191,171, or $36,104 per mile; that of the Boston and Providence, $1,782,000, or $43,460 per mile.

New York, because of its faith in canals and waterways, did not enter on railway building with so much enthusiasm as its sister states to the north and south. In the eight miles of the

Harlem Railroad, however, from near the City Hall "passing along Center and Broome Streets and the Bowery to Fourth Avenue, and thence to Harlem Strait," it could boast the most expensive piece of railway property in America prior to 1839. "The whole cost of the work, including depots, motive and other power, etc., amounted to $1,100,000, or $137,500 per mile."

The New York and Hudson River Railroad had not then been projected, but the construction of the New York and Albany Railroad from "Harlem Strait" to Greenbush, opposite Albany, was under way and was estimated to cost $2,377,946, or nearly $17,000 per mile, "exclusive of land damages, warehouses, locomotives, etc., etc."

"The Erie," commencing on the Hudson River "at Tappan, 25 miles above New York," had been constructed as far as Middletown in Orange county and was already in the throes of financial difficulties. This "stupendous work," as it was called, when completed was to be relinquished "to the state at cost, with interest at 14 per cent. per annum"—which throws a flood of light on the value of money for railroad construction previous to 1839.

The Mohawk and Hudson Railroad, upon which the De Witt Clinton made its trial trip in 1831, connecting Albany with the Erie canal at Schenectady, cost $600,000, or $38,000 per mile.

Original Cost of the Pennsylvania.

The Columbia and Philadelphia Railroad, destined to be the main stem of the great Pennsylvania system, was undertaken by the Keystone state to form a part of the great thoroughfare to Pittsburg and the western states. A description of the journey in early days has been given in the preceding pages. Its construction was authorized by the legislature in 1828 and in October, 1834, it was completed as a double track road the entire way from Philadelphia to Columbia on the Susquehanna river, where the travelers betook themselves to boats. When in 1834 the road was opened for public use, the historian says, "The depots, workshops and other necessary structures, were subsequently completed." The cost of the road without these incidentals in 1834 was as follows:

Cost of the Columbia and Philadelphia Railway in 1834—81.60 Miles:

Grading	$ 649,158.69
Culverts	74,113.94
Viaducts or railway bridges	327,695.80
Roads and farm bridges	42,055.00
Fencing	65,410.86
Railway superstructure,	2,181,156.25
Building and Machinery	111,787.12
Engineering and superintendence	133,934.31
Damages	54,833.29
Repairs	42,451.76
Incidentals	11,980.18
Alteration to accommodate the city of Lancaster	60,000.00
Total	$3,754,577.20

To which there was subsequently added the following items:

Locomotive engines	$ 327,203.41
Additional buildings, turnouts	37,511.16
Retained percentage on former contracts	5,134.08
New ropes at inclined planes	11,584.34
Embankment at Maul's bridge	1,796.34
Renewal of wooden track	18,907.48
Rebuilding Valley Creek bridge destroyed by fire	17,218.13
New road to avoid Columbia inclined plane	118,123.53
Grand Total	$4,296,796.92
Per mile	53,047.00

FIRST LOCOMOTIVE USED ON PENNSYLVANIA RAILROAD.

In the details of these accounts it appears that locomotives cost $6,720 each, and the cars, which were the property of private individuals, $2,000 for passenger and $275 for freight cars. Although the state furnished the steam motive power, provision was made for horse power by laying a "horse path" of broken stone from 6 to 9 inches deep. The owners of the cars paid toll to the state and collected 4 cents a mile from passengers and 9-14/100 cents per mile for a ton of goods.

Two items in the above statement are especially instructive —that for alterations to accommodate Lancaster and that for the new road to avoid Columbia inclined plane. It is impossible to estimate the cost of changes made in American railway routes to accommodate various communities, or of new construction to remedy original misconstruction in levels and alignments, as the field broadened.

Cost of the Alleghany Portage Road.

What was known as the Alleghany Portage Railroad formed the link between the Pennsylvania canal system at Hollidaysburg on the east and the resumption of water transportation at Johnstown on the west, attaining an elevation of 2491 feet above the Atlantic Ocean. The viaduct over the Conemaugh at the Horseshoe bend, described as a "magnificent structure," cost $54,562. The general statement of the cost of this important pioneer work was as follows:

Grading	$472,102.59¼
Masonry	116,402.64¼
First track of Railway	430,716.59½
Second track of Railway	362,987.50½
Building machinery, etc., at planes (first set)	151,923.30¼
Ten stationary engines (second ret)	37,779.75
Buildings, etc., for second set of engines	21,048.59
Depots, machine shops, water stations, weighing machines and various works	41,336.66¼
Total	$1,634,357.69¼
Per mile, 36.96 miles	44,545.00

The fractions of a cent in this statement illustrate the exactness with which the state kept its books in those days, but neglects to throw any light on the cost of the four locomotives used on the "long level" of the road. Nor does the statement cover office expenses, engineering and extra allowances made to contractors by the legislature. This work was completed in 1834.

The initial cost of the Philadelphia and Reading Railroad, including the extension to Pottsville, 95 miles, was $5,000,000, or $52,630 per mile.

Cost in the Forties.

In 1840, when there were 2,818 miles of railway in the United States, an estimate based on earnings and on current publications would indicate that the capital cost, ten years after the opening of the Baltimore and Ohio road, of all the railways in the country was less than $66,000,000 or about $23,000 a mile. This estimate, judged by figures given above, is probably far below the mark. Money for such risky business was worth at least 10 per cent. at that time. More than half of

Freight Engine, 1844.

the mileage of 1840 was in the Middle States, about one-fifth of it in the New England States and not one hundred miles of it was west of the Alleghanies. It was of the most primitive and temporary construction, laid with the strap rail already described and built piecemeal to connect established communities at the least possible cost. Already the railways had been crippled and their extension retarded by the financial panic of 1837. One of the effects of this business recession was the financial embarrassment of the founder of the Baldwin Locomotive Works, who was forced to a settlement with his creditors before continuing his great industry, which has been so intimately associated with the fortunes of American railways since their infancy.

On December 6, 1845, a committee of citizens of Vicksburg appointed to solicit charters from the legislatures of Alabama and Mississippi for the Charleston and Western Railroad (Alabama and Vicksburg now) made the following statement in their report:

"Twenty years ago, a short road at Quincy, to carry marble, was all the pioneer we had. Now, we have nearly 4,000 miles of railroad in actual daily operation in the United States, and a great deal more in the rest of the world. The materials of experience are therefore sufficiently abundant. The cost of 79 railroads in the United States is given in the table published in the American Railroad Journal. The aggregate length of them is 3,723 miles, and the cost is $109,841,460; or $29,325.85 per mile.

"In the Carolinas and Georgia 785¼ miles cost but $14,063,175, or $17,919 per mile; those of North Carolina and Georgia 583¼ miles long, cost $8,391,723; or $14,387.72 per mile; those of Georgia 337¾ miles, cost $5,231,723, or $15,489 per mile; the Central Railroad in Georgia, 190¼ miles, cost $2,551,723; or $13,570.72 per mile; and that part of the Georgia Railroad of 65 miles, which has been constructed of late years, is said to have cost less than $12,000 per mile, including an edge rail; or, as commonly called, a T-rail.

"The residue of the railroads on the list, in the northern and

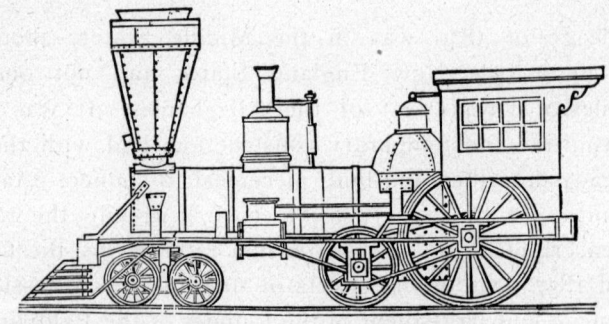

BALDWIN FAST PASSENGER ENGINE, 1848

eastern states, amounting to 2,937¾ miles in length, cost $95,788,295; or $32,633.23 per mile.

"The reason of this difference of cost, in favor of the southern states, is mainly in the abundance and cheapness of timber, the absence of rock excavations, and the low cost of right of way."

The company applying for these charters was to fix and publish its tolls not subject to change "oftener than once a year," with a restriction that the annual profit should not exceed "25 per cent." In those days legislators were only too glad to promise the railways the earth if investors could thereby be tempted to furnish capital to provide much needed transportation.

Cost in the Fifties.

By 1850 the mileage of American railways had risen to 9,021 miles and their earnings were in the neighborhood of $4,000 a mile. An estimate places their cost at this period at $272,-000,000, or over $30,000 per mile. The increase in cost per mile between 1840 and 1850 was largely due to the reconstruction of entire lines to carry the unexpected burden of freight which was beginning to leave the canals and waterways for the more expeditious and accessible railways. During this decade eastern roads began replacing their strap rails with T-rails,—selling their strap rails to western roads for whatever they could get, up as high as $50 a ton—about 30 tons being the average weight to the mile. At this date there were only 131 miles of rails west of Indiana, of which Illinois boasted 111 and Wisconsin 20. It was not until five years later that the great commonwealth of Iowa appeared in a table of railway states. Chicago had not then been reached by rail from the East, the original Michigan Central terminating at New Buffalo, whence its business was transported by steamers across Lake Michigan. Between 1848 and 1850 the railway mileage west of the Alleghanies was almost doubled and then ensued that rush of construction which only suffered temporary abatement during the trying days of the Civil War.

I deem myself fortunate, for the purpose of this record, that there has come into my possession a collection of engineers' reports, covering the period between 1846 and 1854, giving valuable data of estimates and cost of railway construction when the pioneer work was being pushed with great energy into virgin territory. For the benefit of the stockholders of a projected Canadian road one of these reports contains the following statistics of the principal railroads of the two well settled states of New York and Massachusetts in 1851:

NEW YORK AND MASSACHUSETTS RAILWAYS IN 1851.

ITEM.	New York.	Massachusetts.
Length of main lines, miles............................	1,703	1,005
Length of double track, miles........................	346	267
Length of branches, miles............................	56	110
Aggregate length as single line......................	1,992	1,293
Total cost..	$91,423,040	$65,855,315
Average cost per mile, single line....................	45,895	50,930
Average speed passenger trains, miles per hour........	32	24
Average speed freight trains, miles per hour..........	17	13
Average charge per mile, per passenger, first class....	3 cents	3 cents
Total miles run by trains............................	4,738,784	4,726,017
Total passengers carried in cars.....................	8,045,708	9,569,470
Total passengers carried one mile....................	247,878,040	157,202,590
Total tons of freight carried in cars.................	1,274,649	2,499,953
Total tons of freight carried one mile................	75,867,747	76,244,739
Average number of passengers per train..............	66½	55
Average number of tons freight per train.............	40½	50
Total earnings......................................	$10,192,445	$8,786,440
Earnings per mile per annum........................	5,795	9,030
Earnings per mile run...............................	2.10	1.78
Total expenses......................................	4,626,535	4,751,830
Expenses per mile run...............................	90 cents	96 cents
Ratio expenses to income............................	45.4%	53%
Net profit...	$5,565,910	$4,034,610
Profit on cost.......................................	6.1%	6.1%

If the cost per mile had been calculated in the usual way, viz., per mile of line, the cost in New York would have amounted to $52,000 per mile and in Massachusetts to $59,000.

Although the rate per ton mile is not given, it is clear that it must have been approximately 3.67 cents, or not far from 5 times the present rate. Three-quarters of the earnings was from passenger traffic. In 1906 over 70 per cent. of the gross earnings of American railways was from freight.

The ratio of expenses to income of 45.4 per cent. in New York, or even 53 in Massachusetts, half a century ago may well fill the minds of present day operating officials with envy. But they could do better if rates and fares had not been so mercilessly slashed through the periods of fierce competition that have intervened since 1851.

Details for several New England roads, whose names are still familiar to American ears, throwing further light upon the subject we are considering, appear in another tabular statement, from which the following is extracted:

	Mileage	Average cost per mile	Ratio of expense to earnings	Per Cent of profit on cost
Boston and Lowell............	25.77	$88,000	65	7¼
Boston and Maine.............	74.26	61,565	48	8
Boston and Providence........	41.00	67,000	47	7¼
Boston and Worcester.........	44.63	88,570	55	6¾
Fitchburg....................	50.93	66,620	60	5¾
Old Colony...................	37.25	63,710	75	3½
Western (later Boston and Albany).........	155.40	80,065	44	7½

In 1851 the Western Railroad was found by a committee of stockholders to be in need of heavy expenditures to make good depreciation in structures and equipment all the way from Worcester to Albany. Over $81,000 was needed to renew the wooden bridges that had not then been replaced with iron or steel structures. Rails bought in this country had "already manifested great inferiority of quality," and provision had to be made for their replacement at $45 per ton, 100 tons to the mile. Station buildings were out of repair. "The original stock of Engines furnished for the road was, for the most part, both as to power and efficiency inadequate to its business;" so new ones were purchased raising the expenditures for locomotives to $672,739, with only 59 of all descriptions in service. This made each engine represent a cost of over $11,000. About one-fifth of the cars in the passenger service had only four wheels. A similar proportion of "merchandise cars" were in the same primitive fix. For 906 of these the amount of $532,025 had been expended, which is nearly $600 per car, and the committee recommended an "extraordinary expenditure" of $48,704 to replace worn out "with entire new cars." About the only thing that had not suffered depreciation was the value of the land belonging to the corporation. This the committee found "certainly had not." Even after writing off $216,531 for depreciation, the committee found that the stocks and bonds amounting to $10,469,520, only exceeded its assets, not counting the appreciation of its real estate, by $88,409.

The estimates of the chief engineer of the Cleveland and Pittsburgh Railroad for the 99.84 miles from Cleveland to Wellsville on the Ohio river afford an instructive illustration of the cost of building a railway in what was then the "far west." For one mile of superstructure "with H or inverted T-rail weighing 65 pounds to the yard," the estimate was as follows:

COST OF THE CLEVELAND AND PITTSBURGH.

	Per Mile.
Ballast or gravelling for foundation	$ 700.00
10,560 lineal feet of ground sills 4 x 12 inches, 4 cents per foot	422.40
2,112 lineal feet cross ties, each 8 feet, 6 inches long, 7 x 8 inches, at 16 cents per tie	337.92
4,224 spikes for cross ties, 1,050 lbs., at 6 cents per lb.	63.00
Labor laying timber.	260.00
103 tons of iron (H or inverted T rails, weighing 65 lbs. per yard), at **$63 per ton**.	6,489.00
590 chairs, each 15 lbs., 8,850 lbs. at 3½ cents per lb.	309.75
1,180 bolts for fastening chairs, at 10 cents.	118.00
7,258 spikes for rails, 4,542 lbs. at 6 cents per lb.	272.52
Labor laying iron, etc.	240.00
Total	$9,212.59

The estimate for grading, masonry and bridging was $581,320 and for 6 miles of "turnouts" at $12,000 per mile, $72,000. Only $30,000 was estimated for land damages and 8 per cent. was allowed for contingencies. The total estimate including $328,000 for equipment, stations. shops, etc., was $2,076,201 or $21,000 per mile. The provision for rolling stock was as follows:

12 Locomotives and tenders at $7,500	$90,000
24 Passenger cars at $1,500	36,000
120 Freight cars at $500	60,000
120 Freight cars at $333	40,000
Total	$226,000

In its charter as amended in 1845 the Cleveland and Pittsburgh Railroad was authorized to demand and receive "four cents per mile' for passengers, and "not more than eight cents per mile for freight."

When the road was finally completed in 1853, the estimated cost had been exceeded by nearly a million. Real estate for which $30,000 was estimated was already valued at $164,823. Nearly half the capital had been obtained through subscription to stock and $221,650 charges had been incurred in the sale of the Company bonds. The Company earned dividends from the start, which were paid in stock, the cash being put into construction, "instead of borrowing funds for carrying on that work," as the report states.*

This road played a pioneer part in the building of the West and is now a very important link in the Pennsylvania system west of Pittsburgh.

Contemporaneous with the building of the Cleveland and Pittsburgh other railway pioneers were pushing the construction of the Toledo, Norwalk and Cleveland Railroad, now a part of the Lake Shore and Michigan Southern, and in the language of their first annual report (1852) "were obliged to submit to some sacrifices on our stocks and bonds in order to provide the means of payment." The original cost of this road and also of the Ohio section of the Cleveland and Buffalo Railroad was in the neighborhood of $20,000 per mile. The rails (65 lb. to the yard) for this road cost $36.76 per ton, with $6 added for freight, passenger engines $8,000 each, freight engines $9,500, passenger cars, 1st class, $2,200, 2nd class and postoffice cars, $1,200, freight cars $575 to $700. A modern postal car costs from $6,000 upwards.

In a report on the preliminary surveys of the Cleveland, Columbus and Cincinnati Railroad (1846) there is an interesting discussion as to the merits of the T and Plate rail. The difference in cost was no less than $4,164 per mile, for at that early date 56-lb. iron rails cost $80 per ton delivered in Cleveland. Four wheeled freight cars cost $375 each. Light is

---

*This was regarded as sound "economical policy," and the sequel has proved that it was.

thrown on the general cost of railways in those days by the statement of the engineer in chief that the road from Cleveland to Columbus, owing to the small expense for grading, timber, right of way, etc., "may be made at from one-third to one-half the expense of such roads now existing in the United States." As his estimate for the Cleveland to Columbus road was over $15,000 per mile, he placed the cost of other roads from $30,000 to $45,000 a mile, or considerably below the New York and Massachusetts average. The report of this engineer, C. Williams, lays stress on the "creative power" of a railway, its "ability to produce business, that before did not exist, and would not, but for the means of getting promptly and cheaply to market."

The charter of this company, as amended in 1845, grants to it "power to demand and receive for the transportation of persons and property over said railroad or any part thereof, **such rates as the directors of said company may deem reasonable.**"

The prospectuses and preliminary reports of the engineers of this period almost ignore Chicago and the Northwest as an objective. The Pennsylvania system was already making its way by "links in the Great Central Route to St. Louis." The engineer's report on the third link, the Bellefontaine and Indiana Railroad, was not wholly oblivious to the northwestern possibilities when he wrote, "I cannot close this branch of my report without referring to your communication with the great **northwest**. The railroad now under consideration from Indianapolis to LaFayette is on a direct line **towards** Chicago, and it is intended to open a continuous line by that route. At Chicago it will meet the railroad from Galena."

How roads were financed in those days is suggested in a single paragraph in the first "exhibit" of the Columbia, Piqua and Indiana Railroad (now a division of the Pittsburgh, Cincinnati, Chicago and St. Louis Railway), which says:

"The Company have secured the right of way for nearly the entire road (102 miles) which is estimated to be worth $75,000.

Its entire cost will not exceed $30,000, one-half of which will be liquidated by the stock of the company at par. The property and grounds for depots, station houses and machine shops, belonging to the Company, have been acquired by donation or subscription to the capital stock of the Company, and are valued at $50,000."

The idea that only roads in the east represented an investment by stockholders is refuted by every one of these reports which contain statements similar in effect to the following from the exhibit just cited:

WAYS AND MEANS.

Subscriptions to capital stock by counties and townships....	$238,000
Subscriptions in cash by individuals......................	629,500
Subscriptions in lands..................................	100,000
	$ 967,500
Add issue of first mortgage.............................	600,000
Total..	$1,567,500

The bonds bore interest at 7 per cent. and the first $140,000 were disposed of at par.

Right of way "in most cases was conferred voluntarily, the citizens through whose property the road passes acting in the spirit of men who appreciate the advantages to accrue to themselves, as well as the public, from the construction of the road." And well they might, for every railroad built in those days immediately doubled, and often quadrupled, the value of the land through which it passed.

Beginning in 1850, railway building was assisted and stimulated by land grants in portions of the country least able to provide profitable traffic. Figures relating to these are very incomplete, but in 1897 it was estimated that patents had been issued for 87,915,326 acres. The government lost nothing by these grants, as the price of the alternate sections it retained was increased from $1.25 to $2.50 per acre. Lands so obtained were disposed of by the railways to settlers as rapidly as possible and at reasonable prices. Professor John Bell Sanborn, in Bulletin No. 30 of the University of Wisconsin (1899), says that these "lands have not been the source of wealth to the roads that it is commonly supposed. Even in the case of the largest grants the balance for the whole period is quite small and in many cases the land departments are now a source of expense rather than of revenue." The average price obtained has been under $10 an acre. "Comparing the building of the roads which received land grants," says Professor Sanborn, "with those that did not, it seems that there was no particular need for most of the grants. Unaided roads were built along similar routes even faster than aided ones. The great transcontinental roads, however, probably needed the assistance of aid in the shape of land or bonds to secure their construction at the time they were built."

Whatever the value of these land grants, it went to swell the total irrevocably invested in American railways. In comparatively few instances, as mentioned in the succeeding paragraph, were stocks or bonds issued to represent the millions invested in railways through these grants and public and private donation of right of way, etc.

The first annual "exhibit" of the engineer of the Cincinnati, Union and Ft. Wayne Company (now a part of the Grand Rapids and Indiana) sheds instructive light on the taking of land for stock, in these terms:

"The company has taken lands in subscription for stock under the provisions of the law authorizing the same. They were not taken, however, at fancy prices, but at their cash valuation, ascertained by an appraisement under oath, by an appraiser appointed by the company, who did not include perishable improvements in the valuation, nor did he take into consideration the prospective increase of value of the lands, on account of the construction of the railroad."

The lands taken in this case were mortgaged to secure the bonds upon which funds were obtained to complete the road.

Among the interesting and valuable reports of these early days is the first (January 18, 1853) to the stockholders of the

Racine, Janesville and Mississippi Railroad Company (now a part of the Chicago, Milwaukee and St. Paul). "The total estimated cost of the work, fully equipped and furnished in all departments, is $20,000 per mile amounting, for 67 miles of road, to $1,340,000." A year later the engineer presented the following detailed estimate of cost:

Original estimate of cost of 66 miles of Chicago, Milwaukee and St. Paul in 1854:

ROAD.

Grading, masonry and bridging	$ 342,036.00
6,233 55-100 gross tons rail on track, $78	486,216.90
Chairs and spikes, per mile $600	39,648.00
Ties	58,113.75
Laying track and dressing at $400	26,432.00
Ballasting and raising track	86,710.00
3½ miles turnouts	37,710.00
66.08 miles at $16,296.40 per mile, including turnouts	$1,076,866.65

EQUIPMENT.

8 Locomotives	$72,000	
8 passenger cars	16,800	
4 baggage cars	6,400	
70 freight cars	45,500	
Platform and gravel cars	25,000	
		$ 165,700.00
Depot buildings, engine houses, etc		40,000.00
Engineering, superintendence and agencies		35,000.00
Right of way and fencing $1,000 per mile		66,080.00
66.08 miles at $20,938.96 per mile		$1,383,646.65

The capital for this expenditure consisted of:

Capital stock	$ 670,000
First mortgage bonds	670,000
	$1,340,000

Funds for the preliminary work were derived from subscriptions to capital stock, and the account of disbursements to January 17, 1854, were as follows:

Disbursements.

For construction, including grading, bridging, grubbing and materials furnished...............................	$ 75,227.25
For depot grounds at Racine and Beloit and other real estate	37,887.45
For right of way and fencing............................	25,489.14
For engineering, including preliminary surveys............	8,941.70
For expense, including interest and discount, exchange, surveyors' instruments, office furniture, taxes, expenses in procuring right of way, and general expenses under Commissioners and Board of Directors................	8,285.58
For salaries including attorneys and bookkeepers........	1,183.22
Total......................................	$157,014.34

These reports illustrate better than any formal history can, not only the cost of the early railways in the United States, but the sources from which the funds for their construction were derived and the economy with which such funds were expended. Their cost continued to justify Mr. Tanner's comment in 1840 that "The economy with which most of them have been executed, when compared with the cost of similar works abroad, is matter of surprise to all." The reports during the Fifties all exhibit the same spirit set forth in the first report of the engineer of the North-Western Railroad Company (the link of the Pennsylvania system from Blairsville to Newcastle on the line to Cleveland) as follows:

"The object contemplated by the construction of the road is two-fold—1st, to develop the mineral wealth of the region traversed, and furnish an outlet for the surplus productions of a portion of the state entirely destitute of railroad facilities; and 2d, to open a direct communication between Philadelphia and the Lakes; either of which will fully justify the comparatively small expenditure required."

In this particular instance, the expenditure required was estimated for "grading and bridging $1,375,000, averaging $16,272 per mile" for the 84½ miles and "about an equal amount for the superstructure, equipment, depot, water stations, etc., necessary to put the road in running order."

It has cost many times as much more to place this road through that "rugged and difficult country" in a condition to move the modern millions of freight at modern rates.

Some idea of the railway situation before the war can be had by recalling the fact that the Baldwin Locomotive Works, which in 1906 built 2,666 engines, some weighing as much as 175 tons, produced only 47 in 1855; 59 in 1856; 66 in 1857; 33 in 1858; 70 in 1859 and 83 in 1860, and that they varied from 15 to 28 tons in weight. It is difficult to say which is the more instructive contrast, that between the number, or the weight and consequent power of these engines. The decrease in production in 1858 reflects the effect of the business depression in the preceding year.

Cost Since 1860.

In 1860 the railway mileage of the United States had risen to 30,635, more than one-third of which was west of Pittsburgh. So rapid had been the construction into unprofitable territory that the earnings had increased less than $1,000 per mile over the figures for 1850. A conservative estimate places the cost of constructing this mileage at over $1,000,000,000 or about $33,000 per mile. The banking panic of 1857 had little effect to retard railway expansion beyond increasing the cost of floating loans. By this time the work of relaying the original roads with T-rails was completed, although in 1865 Charles A. Dana, who had been appointed to investigate and report what should be done with the railways that had been seized and used by the government and on which it had spent millions of dollars, in his report to Secretary Stanton said: "Our expenditures upon some of these have been very heavy. For instance, we have added to the value of the road from Nashville to Chattanooga at least a million and a half dollars. When that road was recaptured from the public enemy it was in a very bad state of repair. Its embankments were in many places washed away, its iron was what is known as the U-rail, and was laid in the defective old-fashioned manner, upon longitudinal sleepers, without cross-ties." The government replaced the antique construction with T-rails for its own use but with little intention of making the replacement a permanent improvement.

Incredible as it may seem to our generation, when Abraham Lincoln was elected for his first term there was not a mile of railway in the great states of Minnesota, Kansas and Nebraska and only 23 miles on the whole Pacific coast. In the broad territory between, the Indians and buffaloes still roamed; and most of it had not even been organized into territories, much

BALDWIN ENGINE BUILT IN 1861.

less into the present sovereign states. I wonder if the reader realizes what this means? In his "Conquest of Arid America," William E. Smythe says, "The ninety-seventh meridian divides the United States almost exactly into halves." A glance at the map shows that this meridian cut the Red River of the North, the western boundary of Minnesota, at Grand Forks, and thence passes through the Dakotas, Nebraska, Kansas, Oklahoma and Texas. In 1860, less than half a century ago, this vast half of the United States was without railways except for 23 miles in the environs of San Francisco. To it should be added Minnesota and the portions of the other states named east of the 97th meridian, except Texas, which at that time had some 300 miles, all in the eastern section of the state. Today, including Texas and excluding Minnesota, there are over 61,000 miles of railway in this territory, or double the mileage in the whole United States in 1860; and there is need of as much more if it is to secure anything like the benefits of transportation now enjoyed by that half of the republic east of the 97th meridian.

By 1870, when we reach the period of more trustworthy data, the railway mileage of the United States was 52,898 miles, constructed at an approximated cost of $44,000 per mile. This advance in cost is partly represented in the millions spent in rehabilitating the railways of the Southern States, which had been either destroyed or allowed to go to seed during the civil war,

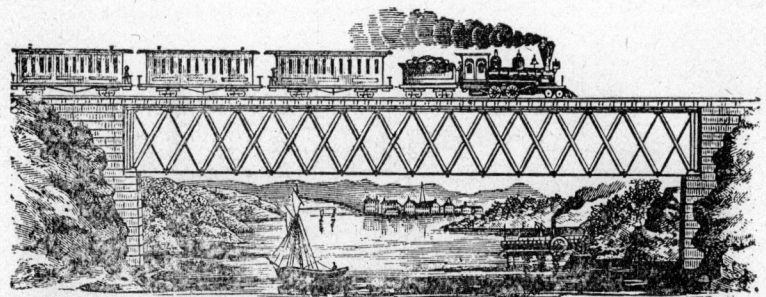

BRIDGE, LOCOMOTIVE, TRAIN AND WOODCUT LANDSCAPE. 1869.

when the mileage in some of these states was at a standstill. Virginia went into the war with 1,379 and came out of it with 1,401 miles; Georgia had 1,420 miles at the beginning and close of the war; Florida, 402 and 416, respectively; Mississippi, 862 and 898; Louisiana, 335 at the opening and close; Kentucky, 549 and 567, respectively; Tennessee, 1,253 and 1,296, and Arkansas did not show a mile of new construction from the opening of the war until 1868. From 1861 to 1865 only 349 miles of railway were constructed in the twelve states in the Southern group, and much of this being for military purposes was of the most flimsy character, to be subsequently abandoned or wholly rebuilt to meet the transportation demands of peace.

Moreover, it was during this period that the Union and Central Pacific Railroads were undertaken and completed at a total cost of over $254,000,000 or $112,000 per mile, with no extravagant expenses for terminals or right of way. The net capitalization of the 2,955 miles owned by the Union Pacific today is less than $85,000 per mile. The building of these two connecting roads, to which the government contributed its credit by issuing over $53,000,000 in 6 per cent. currency bonds, and generous land grants, was then regarded as a patriotic necessity, and its completion in 1869 was celebrated as a proper subject for national rejoicing. In 1869 public sentiment had not been studiously perverted into an attitude of mistrust and hostility toward the one agency that had done more than any other to build up and preserve the Union. The cost of these two roads alone was equivalent to adding $5,000 per mile to the average cost of the entire mileage of the United States.

A GOLD MEDAL AMERICAN ENGINE—PARIS, 1867.

Justice in the public mind has never been done—probably never will be—to the courage, enterprise and indomitable energy of the Americans who pushed this great work through financial shoals and physical obstructions to completion. It and the Central Pacific, as well, were built at war prices. Labor was scarce and was to be had only at exorbitant figures. The cost of materials was well nigh prohibitive. The price of ties laid down at Omaha ran as high as $2.50. The rails for the first 440 miles of the Union Pacific cost $135 per ton. When railway connection was established between Council Bluffs and the East this was reduced to $97.50. Government bonds were issued as the work progressed, and netted the Company only 65 cents on the dollar. The country through which it was built was the hunting ground of the most warlike Indians of the West. They harrassed the work at every stage, from scalping surveying parties to attacks on graders, who worked with their guns stacked within easy reach. It is related that more than half the construction gangs were men who had been through the war, which experience stood them in good stead.

The conception of this work was an inspiration of patriotism; its financiering was a nightmare; its physical construction was a battle between civilization and the forces of savagery and Nature, worthy the pen of Fenimore Cooper; its progress was a titanic race for subsidies and its completion was hailed with patriotic acclaim throughout the Union. President Lincoln designated the eastern terminus of this transcontinental railway on March 7, 1864, and on May 10, 1869, President Grant received the tidings that the last spike—a golden one from California—had been driven that joined the rails of the Union and Central Pacific Railways at Promontory, Utah. That event was celebrated in a poem by Bret Harte beginning:

What was it the engines said,
Pilots touching head to head;
Facing on the single track
Half a world behind each back.

And what was this great work whose completion marked the meeting of the iron girdle across a continent, with half a world behind each pilot? It was a hastily graded, unballasted, indifferently equipped, single track road of 1921 miles, laid with 56-lb. iron rails, through sparsely settled deserts and mountains, which, paradoxical as it may seem, cost three times as much as it was worth and yet was worth more than three times as much as it cost.

The Union Pacific of 1907 has more miles of yard track and sidings than the Union Pacific of 1870 had miles of main line.

It was between 1860 and 1870 that the steel rail first made its appearance and began to supplant iron on roads whose traffic justified the cost of its substitution. That this was almost prohibitive for weak roads may be judged from the fact that in 1870 the price of steel rails was still $106 per ton. The first steel rails used in the United States cost $210 per ton, and the Pennsylvania Railroad paid $206 per ton for the first Bessemer steel rails which it laid in 1865.

By 1880 the mileage of operated railways in the United States had increased to 82,146 and the cost per mile had risen to over $56,000. No one at all conversant with the history of American railways during the preceding decade will be at a loss to account for this development. It covered a period of extraordinary expansion, disaster and recovery. Between 1870 and 1873 nearly 18,000 miles of road had been built, more than 10,000 miles of which was in the sparsely settled western states where construction was expensive, population was needed and traffic was light. The Northern Pacific Railroad, for which ground was broken in 1870, boasted that it was going into a territory that "would make ten States as large as Pennsylvania, **wholly unsupplied with railroads."** In the language of Poor's Manual, speaking of one western road, "Nearly the whole increase of mileage has proved unproductive." This was true of all other western railroads. It was simply a case of excess of mileage to population. The country was railroad mad, and then, as ever, speculative promoters took advantage of the fever to project lines into territory which could not be expected to support them for another decade. Then came the granger legislation in the same western states, which frightened capital and effectually put an end to railway expansion, until, with its modification or repeal by 1878, there came restored confidence and renewed activity in building into the wilderness, soon to be peopled with millions brought thither by the railways which looked to the future to recompense them for what were origi-

"Monster of 1876" (3 ft. 6 in. Gauge) and a Modern Locomotive.

nally unprofitable optimistic ventures. How the financial and industrial panic of 1873 affected the railways is shown in the receiverships during the following years, a summary of which is given elsewhere (page 154). Its effect upon the cost of the railways is reflected in the advance from a cost of $44,000 per mile in 1870 to $56,000. While the panic and liquidation wiped out millions of dollars of investments, it simply created the necessity of raising other millions to restore many roads which were permitted to run down and to bring others up to the higher standard required by our increasing population and expanding trade. Roadbed, bridges, rails, equipment and terminal facilities had to undergo a complete transformation to meet the demands of a freight traffic that more than doubled in ten years.

Between 1870 and 1880 the mileage of secondary track and sidings had more than doubled, and, while steel rails were so exceptional in 1870 as to escape the attention of the statistician, by 1880 there were 33,679 miles of line laid with steel. The substitution of steel rails for iron during this decade alone at prices ranging from $106 per ton in 1870 to $57 in 1880, cannot have cost the railways of the United States during the period in question less than $250,000,000, or over $3,000 per mile.

Between 1880 and 1889 no less than 15,570 miles of track were converted from a gauge of 5 feet or over to the standard American 4 feet $8\frac{1}{2}$ inch gauge. Before 1886 there had been an infinite confusion of gauges varying from 2 feet up to 6 feet, with over 3,000 miles with two separate gauges.

In 1890 we arrive at the period of official figures of cost of construction given in the first table in this chapter. Unfortunately, it was not until 1892 that the official statistician included in his report a statement of the miles of line represented in this cost. Assuming that 140,000 miles were represented it would appear that the cost of construction up to that date was $55,000 as against $56,000 in 1880. This decrease in the average was due to the construction in ten years of over 40,000 miles of comparatively inexpensive lines in the territory west of the east line of Illinois and the Mississippi River. The magnificent territory of the Northwest and Southwest only needed the railways to make them accessible for the thousands of settlers who waited on transportation to convert it into the great agricultural and industrial states it has since become. How some of these states have profited by the empire building railroad construction of the twenty years before 1890 is shown in the following statement:

	Miles of Railroad 1870.	Miles of Railroad 1890.	Increase.
Iowa	2,683	8,347	5,664
Minnesota	1,092	5,466	4,374
Kansas	1,501	8,806	7,305
Texas	711	7,911	7,200
North Dakota	65	1,940	4,360
South Dakota		2,485	
Colorado	157	4,154	3,997
Total	5,209	39,109	32,900

Railways at any cost were indispensable to the very states which were among the first to disregard the scripture injunction, "Thou shalt not muzzle the ox when he treadeth out the corn." It is worth remembering that the population of these states increased from 2,970,749 in 1870 to 7,799,505 in 1890. It is difficult to imagine any of these states dependent on waterways and post roads.

During the following decade to 1900 the reported cost of construction rose to $10,263,313,400 for 181,437 miles represented, or over $56,500 per mile. This shows an increase per mile over both 1880 and 1890, and is easily accounted for by the continued transformation and improvement that was going on throughout the railway world. Where over 74,000 miles of new road had been built between 1880 and 1890, less than 37,000 were added to the total mileage in the succeeding decade. In the meantime, however, the auxiliary tracks and sidings had increased from 33,711 to 52,153 miles; the tracks laid with steel rails increased from 167,458 miles to 238,464 and covered 92.4 per cent of the total trackage of the country; the adoption of automatic couplers and train brakes scarcely begun in 1890 had become well nigh universal; various forms of block signal systems were being installed and the whole railway transportation system had been put on a plane of efficiency beyond the anticipations of 1890. The proof of this increased efficiency is found in the following statement of the public service rendered in 1890 and 1900:

	1900.	1890.
Passengers carried...............................	576,865,230	492,430,865
Passengers carried one mile.......................	16,039,007,217	11,847,785,617
Passengers carried one mile, per mile of line.........	83,295	75,751
Tons of freight carried............................	1,101,680,238	636,541,617
Tons of freight carried one mile....................	141,599,157,270	76,207,047,298
Tons of freight carried one mile per mile of line......	735,366	487,245

Here is an increase of over 35 per cent. in passenger service and nearly 86 per cent. in freight service during a decade when the population of the republic showed a growth of less than 21 per cent. The marvel of this achievement is that it was effected in the face of one of the worst periods of reaction experienced in the industrial progress of the United States, to which reference has already been made. Even in 1900 $3,176,609,698 of railway stocks outstanding, or 54.34 per cent. of the gross capital stock **paid no dividends.**

The country recovered from the effects of the slump of 1893 more rapidly than the railways, which were forced to extraordinary expenditures to make good the depreciation in road and equipment suffered during the receiverships and enforced economies of 1893-1897. And during this period of recovery the railways were called on to make provision for transporting traffic which increased at a pace unparalleled in the previous history of the country, although it has been surpassed since.

The analysis of the cost of construction at the date of the latest official statistics requires a separate chapter.

VI

PRESENT COST OF ROAD AND EQUIPMENT

In his balance sheet for the year ending June 30, 1905, the official statistician gives the following statement of the cost of road and equipment for "203,228 miles of line."

	Amount 1905.	Increase over 1904.
Cost of road...	$11,170,458,581	$ 389,288,643
Cost of equipment.................................	780,890,368	46,889,612
Total.................................	$11,951,348,949	$436,178,255
Per mile of line...................................	$58,809	

Unfortunately for my purpose this balance sheet bears on its face evidence of its own incompleteness. Its statement of liabilities places the capital stock at $6,680,473,280 and the funded debt at $7,568,555,810, aggregating $14,249,029,090 for "203,228 miles of line represented." As the total railway capital for 209,405 miles of line in another summary of the same report is given at $13,805,258,121,, the total in the balance sheet is manifestly incorrect. This error is all the more bewildering because the statistician in connection with the lesser total says:

"The aggregate railway capital at the close of the year was $13,805,258.121, which is equal to a par capitalization of $65,926 per mile of line. This assignment makes no deduction of stocks and bonds owned by railways in their corporate capacity, and to the extent that such deductions are proper, overstates the capital per mile of line."

An examination of earlier balance sheets shows that this discrepancy, by which the capitalization of a part of the railways is made to exceed the whole, has been steadily growing since 1898. Prior to that date the balance of capital was always very properly on the side of the greater mileage, even though the capital per mile of line was not.

Another feature of this balance sheet, calculated to detract from its authority, is that in the list of assets the stocks and bonds owned by the railways are given as follows:

STOCKS AND BONDS OWNED 1905 GIVEN IN BALANCE SHEET.

	Amount 1905.	Increase over 1904.
Stocks owned	$1,766,761,049	$ 43,539,611
Bonds owned	572,609,132	14,216,048
Total	$2,339,370,171	$57,755,659

Compare these figures with the following from the summary of ownership of railway stocks and bonds, page 56 of the same report:

STOCKS AND BONDS ACTUALLY OWNED.

	Amount owned by Railway Corporations. 1905.	Increase over 1904.
Stocks	$2,070,052,108	$127,193,749
Bonds	568,100,021	9,627,779
Total	$2,638,152,129	$136,821,528
Discrepancy	298,781,958	79,065,869

These discrepancies cannot be explained as due to the difference in mileage represented in the summaries and the balance sheet, for the excess of capital in the balance sheet is for less mileage, and itself proves that all the great stock and bond owning companies are included in the balance sheet.

Such discrepancies would be immaterial for the purposes of this inquiry did they not tend to discredit the two items of the balance sheet in which we are interested. Here again the inquirer after truth is confronted with a statement of cost of equipment that strains credulity. The official balance sheet places the cost of equipment in 1905 at $780,890,368 and the increase in such cost at $46,889,612. Turning to the section of the official report relating to equipment for that year, it appears that the railways owned 48,357 locomotives, 40,713 cars in passenger service, 1,731,409 freight cars and 70,749 work cars. The exact expenditure on account of this equipment is not known,

1880—Passenger Coaches—1905.

but if it had to be replaced today its cost might safely be estimated at the prices given in the following computation:

Number and Cost of Equipment in 1905.

	Average Cost.	Aggregate Cost.
48,357 locomotives at	$12,000	$580,204,000
40,713 passenger cars at	6,000	244,278,000
1,731,409 freight cars at	1,000	1,731,409,000
70,749 work cars at	600	42,449,400
Total		$2,598,340,400

From which it is evident that the cost of equipment as given in the official balance sheet is less than one-third what it should be. The estimated cost of the several items in this table could be reduced to $10,000; $5,000; $800 and $400 respectively and the total cost would still be $2,100,561,800, or nearly 170 per cent. more than the total given by the official statistician.

Unfortunately, it is not permissible to correct the official balance sheet by substituting an estimate, however reasonable, in place of an error, however palpable, or the cost of construction would read as follows:

Cost of road...	$11,170,458,581
Cost of equipment, estimated.........................	2,598,340,400
Total cost of construction.............................	$13,768,798,981

or with a reduced estimated cost per item, as follows:

Cost of road...	$11,170,458,581
Cost of equipment.......................................	2,100,561,800
Total cost of construction.............................	$13,271,020,381

But railway accounts have been so lacking in uniformity and have come through so many vicissitudes and reorganiza-

STEEL PASSENGER CAR, 1907—TOTAL WEIGHT, 105,500 LBS.

tions that there is absolutely no way by which we can test the "Cost of road" items. As given in the "Balance Sheet," there is every probability that it includes many millions of dollars expended on cost of equipment. But on the other hand there is an equal probability that it excludes other millions of cumulative cost expended through seventy odd years of railway development out of income for additions, betterments and improvements.

Fortunately, there is independent data by which to arrive at a more accurate approximation of the cost of construction of American railways than is afforded by the official "Balance Sheet." In 1906, official reports from 313 companies operating 206,960 miles of line, or approximately 94 per cent. of the aggregate mileage in the United States, furnished the following data in regard to their actual cost for 166,493 miles owned to June 30th of that year:

	Line represented, 166,493 Miles.
Cost of road	$5,966,303,567
Cost of equipment	786,469,647
Cost of both, not separated	3,286,313,826
Total cost of construction	$10,039,087,040

Distributing the third item in this table between cost of road and equipment in the same proportion as that where they were separately reported, it was found that the total cost of road would be $8,874,691,398 and of equipment $1,164,395,642.

The 313 companies operated 40,477 miles of line under leases in one form or another, for which they paid $116,144,978 rental. Estimating that they paid as high as 10 per cent. on the cost of these leased lines, much of which was for essential terminal trackage, would make a capitalized cost of $1,161,949,780. To this should be added the cost of 13,066 miles of unreported line, for which $30,000 per mile is a low estimate. Adding to these the estimate of actual cost of equipment in 1906 already made gives the following statement of the cost of constructing and equipping 220,036 miles of line in 1906:

Cost of 220,036 Miles of Line Operated.

Cost of road (166,493 miles) owned	$8,874,691,398
Cost of road (40,477 miles) leased	1,161,949,780
Cost of road (13,066 miles unreported, at $30,000)	391,980,000
Cost of equipment	2,758,611,600
Total cost of construction	$13,187,232,778

It will be perceived that by following an independent route we arrive at approximately the same results—the higher total of the table derived from the official Balance Sheet being undoubtedly due to the inclusion therein of cost of equipment under cost of road.

Whichever figures we accept, it is evident that the bookkeeping cost of constructing the railways of the United States is in the neighborhood of $13,000,000,000. This is $1,328,059,351 more than their net capitalization in 1906!

The reason why the original cost of construction is an item that cannot generally be ascertained, "except for relatively new roads," is thus admirably stated by the Railroad Commission of Wisconsin in its decision in fixing the passenger fare in that state at $2\frac{1}{2}$ cents per mile:

"Most of the roads were built by construction companies whose records are not in existence, and then turned over to some other company at a different value than the original cost. Many of the roads are undergoing constant improvements; in fact, some of them have been almost entirely rebuilt since the time of their first construction. The original cost as well as the amount that has been expended upon the plant to any given date, exclusive of the maintenance, are items that for these and other reasons cannot be obtained, and which would probably be of little value if they could be had."

There is little reason to doubt, however, that the $13,000,000,000 the "bookkeeping cost of construction" fairly represents the amount of money that between 1830 and 1906 has been expended in bringing the railways of America up from the 23 miles of experiments with horses and 7-ton engines for motive power, to the 309,218 miles of track upon which engines weighing as high as 175 tons drag trains carrying an average of 322

BALDWIN MALLET COMPOUND, 1906. WEIGHT ON DRIVERS, 350,000 LBS.

tons of freight. At every step money has been spent that has never appeared in the construction account, some of it on roads that have disappeared from the map; much of it has gone in driblets—here an additional spike, there one more tie per rail; here a hundred feet of siding, there miles of double track; everywhere betterments and improvements charged to operating expenses or paid for out of surplus income, amounting in some instances to more than the dividends and often where no dividends were declared.

Cost Measured by Traffic.

The extent and cost of the improvements during three-quarters of a century cannot be ascertained, but it can be measured by the growth in the volume of traffic. The type of the physical structure of the railway, the strength of its track and bridges, the length of its auxiliary track, the character and cost of its depots, freight houses and shops, the quality of its service—everything in fact that contributes to its value as a public servant—depends on the amount of its traffic. The cost of the instrument, commensurate to the traffic it has handled, has paralleled the growth of that traffic.

So late as 1851, the total tonnage of all the railways of the United States is stated to have been less than 5,000,000 tons, from which the receipts were $20,192,104, or over $4 per ton, irrespective of distance.

In 1906, the total freight carried by the railways of the United States was 1,631,374,219 tons, for which the receipts were $1,640,386,655, or $1.01 per ton, irrespective of distance.

If the railways of 1906 had received the same rate per ton charged by those of 1851 their freight receipts would have exceeded $6,500,000,000 instead of the one-fourth of that sum they actually earned.

Between 1851 and 1906 the mileage of American railways covered in the above data increased from 8,876 to 222,340 miles, that is, 25 fold.

But their tonnage in the meantime increased from 5,000,000 to 1,631,374,219 tons, that is to say 326 fold, or over 13 times faster than their mileage.

To handle this remarkable increase in volume of traffic of 13 times per mile, the cost of road and equipment has only risen from about $30,000 per mile in 1850 to about $60,000 in 1906, while the net capitalization has only increased to $54,421.

In other words, transportation capacity in fifty years has increased over 1,000 per cent., while the cost of the medium has increased 100 per cent. per mile and the capitalization of the medium has increased less than 75 per cent. per mile.

FAST MAIL, 1904—TAKEN INSTANTANEOUSLY WHILE RUNNING 80 MILES AN HOUR.
GREEN, PHOTOGRAPHER.

Accompanying this wonderful achievement and inseparably involved with it has been the still more amazing phenomenon of a decrease in the cost of railway service to the public, amounting in the case of freight rates to nearly 80 per cent. and in passenger rates to at least 33 per cent. and to fully 66 per cent. from the pre-railway days.

That these estimated reductions in the cost of railway service to the public are not wide of the mark is proved by the reports of the Pennsylvania Railroad. Since as late as 1864 its average earnings per ton mile have declined from 2.498 cents to 0.595 in 1906, or 76 per cent., and its passenger receipts from 2.672 cents to 2.014, or over 24 per cent. Had the Pennsylvania received the same rates in 1906 that it did in 1864 its freight earnings last year would have been over $460,000,000 instead of only $109,960,888, and its passenger earnings would have been nearly $40,000,000 instead of only $30,074,868. Today the cost of road of the Pennsylvania Railroad is $134,000 per mile of road owned and of equipment $17,000 per mile of line operated. In 1864 the cost of its road and equipment was $81,000 per mile of owned road. In 1906 the freight service of the Pennsylvania was over 40 times greater than in 1864 and its passenger service was nine fold greater, while the cost to the public has been at the reduced rates as above stated.

The actual cost of reconstructing, equipping and expanding the Pennsylvania road to meet the demands of a traffic more than doubling every decade, in the nature of railway service cannot be ascertained. But that it exceeds the book account of cost of construction many millions admits of no doubt. Spectacular expenditures, like that of tunneling Manhattan Island, perfecting its Philadelphia terminal and reducing its grades through the Alleghanies, halt public attention and get into the capital account in sums of eight figures, but of the million and one items of improvement going on constantly, all charged in the day's work, so to speak, who knows or can compute them? Financiers know that since 1899 the Pennsylvania has invested $72,941,000 in betterments and charged it to income, paid off $17,020,000 Car Trust obligations out of profits and invested $42,649,000 premiums on stock issued in improvements, but even they have no means of knowing how much has gone into the cost of the railways and been charged to operating expenses.

During the eight years 1899 to 1906 inclusive, no less than $274,816,000 has been expended by the Pennsylvania Railroad on additions and improvements, nearly half of which was derived from profits as shown in the accompanying statement:

BETTERMENTS AND OUTLAYS OUT OF PROFITS.

Year to Dec. 31.	Additions to Cost of Road and Equipment Charged Capital	Betterments and Sinking Funds	Car Trust Capital Payments	Other Sums used to meet Capital Expenditures
1906	$33,532,000	$11,558,000	$4,246,000	$15,201,000
1905	38,832,000	8,739,000	3,249,000	....
1904	12,199,000	6,809,000	3,249,000	....
1903	29,292,000	10,030,000	2,685,000	17,362,000
1902	24,932,000	13,037,000	1,472,000	....
1901	....	11,337,000	1,121,000	8,536,000
1900	1,671,000	8,496,000	585,000	1,550,000
1899	1,748,000	2,935,000	413,000	....
Total	$142,206,000	$72,941,000	$17,020,000	$42,649,000

Expenditures like these have led such high authority as the London **Statist** to remark that "Not only does the capital account of the Pennsylvania Railroad contain no 'water,' but it is doubtful if the road could now be built and equipped up to its present standard for more than double the sum at which it is now capitalized."

What has been done in this way by the Pennsylvania has been the characteristic policy of maintaining structures and equipment on every railway in America that has pretended to keep pace with the expanding traffic requirements of the times. It has been done whether the roads could afford it or not, whether they paid dividends or not, under the inexorable compulsion of their public service.

In its recent investigation into the finances of the Chicago, Milwaukee and St. Paul Railway, the Railroad Commission of Wisconsin found that $25,617,015 or one-tenth of "the cost of the plant" was "represented by surplus earnings and other income which had been devoted to new construction"; and that between June 30, 1899, and June 30, 1906, "about $7,826,758 were charged to operating expenses and credited to the Renewal and Improvement fund." Speaking of the permanent improvements which were included in disbursements before the income account of this road was credited with the surplus, the Railroad Commissioners of Senator La Follette's own state decided that:

"These additions to the plant are undoubtedly in the nature of permanent investments that could have been properly charged to the construction account. The sums thus spent are equities which belong to the stockholders, which they could have taken out in the form of dividends or they could very properly have been added to the surplus."

In passing, it is interesting to note that while the Commissioners found that the cost of construction account of the Chicago, Milwaukee and St. Paul Railway showed $32,247 per mile for the entire line, their estimate of the cost of reproduction of the part of it in Wisconsin was $37,388 per mile. Compare these figures with a net capitalization of only $31,605 per mile!

If the present value of the right of way of the Chicago,

Milwaukee and St. Paul Railway, largely obtained free of charge, were added to its cost of construction, as the Commissioners admitted it very properly might be, the excess of cost to capital of this one road would be in the neighborhood of $10,000 per mile.

Assuming that there is a more or less close relation between cost and capitalization in the different groups into which the country is divided by the Interstate Commerce Commission, the following table of net capitalization and earnings per mile in the several groups shows that capitalization or cost of construction is absolutely without determining effect on the cost of the service to the public:

CAPITALIZATION AND COST OF SERVICE, 1905.

Group.	Miles of Line.	Net Capital per Mile.	Average Passenger Receipts per Mile. Cents.	Average Freight Receipts per Ton Mile. Cents.
I. New England.........	7,980	$53,279	1.762	1.179
II. North Atlantic........	22,100	102,931	1.722	.665
III. Ohio, etc.............	23,915	67,543	1.957	.607
IV. South Atlantic........	12,169	45,770	2.363	.691
V. Central and Gulf	23,869	36,879	2.298	.839
VI. North Central.........	46,836	43,350	1.987	.766
VII. North Western........	11,337	42,069	2.108	.900
VIII. South Western........	29,384	50,557	2.108	.988
IX. Texas..................	14,393	39,099	2.283	1.096
X. Pacific.................	17,422	49,280	2.124	1.098
United States...............	(a) 209,405	$53,328	1.962	.766

(a) Net after deducting line operated under trackage rights.

This table will afford a perplexing study to those theorists who persist in claiming that capitalization exercises a controlling influence on rates. The effect of density and volume of traffic and length of haul is reflected in every figure of this significant table. It also indicates that outside of Groups I and II there is not enough density of passenger traffic to justify a 2 cent maximum fare.

Unfortunately, the official statistics do not furnish data for a like distribution of cost of construction among the several groups. As the cost of construction for the whole country exceeds the net capitalization by about 12 per cent., anyone interested can arrive at an approximation of the cost in any particular group by adding such percentage to its net capitalization per mile. The difference between cost and capital, however, varies greatly in different groups.

The comparative data of the above table leads up to a wider field of comparative statistics.

VII

COMPARATIVE CAPITALIZATION

Candidly considered, nothing in the history of American railways should redound more to their credit than their low capital as compared with either the cost or capitalization of the railways of other countries—unless it be the cheapness of their freight rates. In either or both respects comparisons are odious —to their detractors.

The plain unvarnished facts on this point, from official sources, are presented in the following table:

CAPITAL OR COST OF CONSTRUCTION.

EUROPEAN RAILWAYS.

Year.	Country.	Miles of Line.	Capital or Cost of Construction.	Cost per Mile.
1905	United Kingdom	22,847	$6,247,240,553	$273,438
1903	Russian Europe	30,050	2,833,853,000	94,304
1905	German Empire	34,048	3,486,711,237	102,435
1904	France	24,755	3,313,980,000	133,871
1904	Austria	12,710	1,378,308,847	108,443
1904	Hungary	11,069	695,188,847	62,805
1903	Italy	10,016	1,102,811,500	110,104
1903	Spain	8,559	813,105,000	95,000
1903	Sweden	7,551	230,242,016	30,491
1905	Norway	1,526	57,087,216	37,409
1905	Denmark	1,992	52,352,500	26,281
1904	Belgium	2,520	408,836,500	162,236
1904	Holland	2,060	139,769,000	67,849
1904	Switzerland	2,603	269,083,877	103,374
1904	Bulgaria	751	29,707,000	39,556
1904	Servia	440	24,350,000	55,341
1904	Roumania	1,974	150,579,877	76,281
	Total	175,471	$21,233,206,970	$121,007

Other Parts of the Globe.

1905	Canada........................	21,353	$1,332,498,704	$62,403
1904	British India.................	27,560	1,182,500,000	42,906
1906	Japan.........................	4,488	217,295,827	48,417
1902	Argentine Republic............	10,798	568,000,000	52,602
1905	Mexico........................	6,503	376,181,625	57,847
1906	New Zealand...................	2,406	111,469,900	45,826
1904	Victoria......................	3,371	200,721,920	59,543
1906	New South Wales...............	3,390	212,458,620	62,672
1906	South Australia...............	1,745	66,280,700	37,982
1904	Queensland....................	2,928	101,718,690	34,739
1906	Central South Africa..........	2,158	112,053,255	51,899
1904	Cape Colony...................	2,533	128,830,273	50,861
1905	Natal.........................	783	63,103,239	80,592

The United States.

1906................................	214,475	$11,671,940,649	$54,421

Taken singly or collectively, the obvious comparisons of this table are a triumphant refutation of the charge that American railways are over capitalization.

And when it is considered that they have been constructed by labor whose wages has always been from two to twenty times* higher than the wages paid in other countries, the contrast would pass belief were the figures not incontrovertible.

Cost of British Roads.

An examination into the conditions in the several countries only deepens the first impression of amazement over what has been accomplished in America with low capitalization.

In Great Britain, railways were built from the start in the most substantial manner. The Liverpool and Manchester road, upon which Stevenson made his successful demonstration of the tractive capacity of the locomotive, is said to have cost $4,100,-000, or $100,000 per mile. The rails were of forged iron, 35 pounds to the yard. These rested on cubes of stone let into the ground three feet apart, and the track was amply strong for engines whose original weight was figured not to exceed six tons—the Rocket was only $4\frac{1}{2}$ tons.

---

*In India laborers are paid from 4 to 8 cents per day; in Japan from 10 to 15 cents.

In 1850, when official statistics first took cognizance of British railways as a whole, their capital cost was well over $100,000 per mile. Since 1860 it has steadily risen, as appears from the following table:

Year.	Miles of Line.	Paid-up Capital.	Capital per Mile.
1850	6,621	$1,170,118,528	$176,728
1860	10,433	1,695,293,718	162,493
1870	15,537	2,580,655,237	166,090
1875	16,658	3,069,188,415	184,247
1880	17,933	3,546,903,049	197,786
1885	19,169	3,973,228,727	207,273
1890	20,073	4,370,688,766	217,739
1895	21,174	4,875,406,776	230,254
1900	21,855	5,727,129,204	262,051
1905	22,847	6,247,240,553	273,438

Here we find between 1870 and 1905 an increase of 142 per cent. in capitalization against an increase of only 47 per cent. in mileage. The increased cost amounts to no less than $107,348 per mile, or double the present capitalization per mile of the railways of the United States, and more than that of those of the German Empire.

Nor is this startling increase in the average capitalization of British railways to be accounted for by extraordinary expenditures for double track. The percentage of second track in 1870 was practically the same as in 1905, being 54 per cent. in the former year against 55.5 in the latter.

The explanation of the very high capitalization of British roads is to be found in the heavy cost of right of way owing to the density of population when railway building began, heavy masonry and tunnelling work, and the system adopted in the United Kingdom of charging betterments and improvements to capital account and dividing practically all net receipts among security holders. In 1871 there were 261 persons to the square mile in the Kingdom and no less than 391 in England, or a greater density than that of Massachusetts in 1906. The present density for England and Wales is 558 per square mile.

The initial cost of right of way of British roads indicates what would be the expense of securing right of way in populous territory in the United States today, and has an important bearing on the question of what it would cost to reproduce American roads under twentieth century conditions.

An analysis of the elements of cost of seven of the principal British railways made by the **London Mining Journal** in 1844 gives the following interesting averages:

SEVEN BRITISH RAILWAYS 1844.

(£ = $4.80 then.)

	Cost per Mile.
Parliamentary expenses.	£1,000
Law charges, engineering and direction.	1,600
Land and compensation.	5,000
Railway works and stations.	26,000
Carrying establishment (equipment).	3,000
Total ($175,680).	£36,600

The three leading lines, viz., the London and Birmingham, the Great Western and the Southwestern cost £47,000 ($225,600) per mile, and "the average cost of all the English passenger lines was £34,600 ($166,080)."

Discussing these averages, the **London Mining Journal** said: "The United States had 3,500 miles of railway open in 1839. None of these cost more than £10,000 per mile, and the average of the whole was only £4,800. It is true some of these are single, and others are of slight construction; **but it is a startling fact that the best American railways, which are said to be little inferior to ours, are made at one-third the expense.**"

The attention of the reader is called to the item of £5,000 in the above table for "Land and Compensation." It will be perceived that it exceeds the entire average cost of American railways in 1839. Many early railways in the United States were built and equipped for less than the average sum paid by British roads for parliamentary, legal and engineering charges. It will also be observed that less than one-twelfth of the cost of British roads was invested in equipment. Of the chief item, £26,000 ($124,800) for "railway works and stations," the same London publication above quoted said:

"Useless expense, too, has often been incurred in the execution of railways from the ambition of engineers to render the works monuments of their own skill by making all the parts unnecessarily strong or unnecessarily perfect."

The engineers of British railways laid them out and constructed them as if they were building for eternity and already knew all the demands the future was to put upon their work. American engineers confronted a different problem in a different and wiser spirit. They suited their plans to their generation, recognizing that transportation on this continent was in its infancy, and that nothing they could do, with the capital and experience at their command, could possibly anticipate the star of empire in its western flight over what in 1839 was mostly wilderness.

The monumental British roads of 1844, reconstructed up to date, would be ground to dust beneath the traffic which daily passes over the leading American lines. This is no mere figure of speech, for the best British construction of today has been tested on the Pennsylvania road and found wanting in stability under 90 and 100 ton engines drawing loads of 1,000 tons and upwards.

In passing it may be said that the Great Western Railway mentioned above as one of the leading British roads had a 7-foot gauge down to 1892, and that the London and North-Western Railway, which swallowed the London and Birmingham also referred to above, has a paid up capital of £122,662,484, or over $347,508 per mile. The Midland Railway, however, surpasses this with $404,366 per mile.

As if to further emphasize the contrast in capitalization between British and American railways it may be said that our locomotives average more than twice as heavy, while our freight cars average 33 tons capacity to under 12 tons for theirs.

Today the railways of the United States are capitalized at less than one-fifth the paid up capitalization of British railways.

Cost of German Railways

At all stages the capital cost of the railways of Germany has been about double that of American railways, and less than half that of British roads. From such data as is available the following statement of their cost at different periods is submitted:

Year.	Miles of Line.	Cost.	Cost per Mile.
1868	10,600	$823,030,000	$77,644
1870	11,730	993,480,000	84,695
1880	20,690	2,098,970,000	101,448
1888	24,270	2,410,650,000	99,326
1895	*28,071	2,777,487,620	98,945
1900	30,956	3,025,111,981	97,723
1905	34,048	3,486,711,237	102,435

*Since 1895, inclusive, the figures are official; prior to that they are Mulhall's.

The increase in mileage and cost per mile between 1870 and 1880 is significant of the change that took place under the consolidating hand of Bismarck. It unified German railways at an increased cost of over $16,000 per mile.

The reasons why the cost of German railways is less than that of British are four fold—labor is cheaper there, population is not (especially was not) so dense, the physical problem was easier and they were not so well built. They were more expensive than American roads despite the cheaper labor and easy engineering because of the density of the population and the costly bureaucratic methods of construction.

The average daily wages of an unskilled laborer in Germany in 1840 was about 32 cents against 49 cents in England and 90 cents in the United States. Relatively wages in the several countries have remained about the same ever since; in Germany ranging from 48 cents to 75 cents now, in Great Britain from 60 to 85 cents and in the United States from $1.25 to $1.75. In the working of railways the three systems are confronted with the same difference in the cost of labor which absorbs 60 per cent. of all operating expenses.

In 1837 the territory now included in the German Empire had a population of 31,589,547, or 151 persons to the square mile, where, about the same time, England and Wales had 273; Massachusetts in 1840 had 92, and the whole United States only 8.4 per square mile. In 1900 Germany had a density of 270 to the square mile, or still only about half that of England, but ten times greater than that of the United States.

The cost of constructing the railways of Germany was very

much less than in Great Britain by reason of the topography of the country. Speaking of this feature of the difference in cost Edwin A. Pratt, in his "German vs. British Railways," says:

"Between the Hook of Holland and Berlin the railway does not pass through a single tunnel (there is in fact not a single railway tunnel in the whole of North Germany), nor does it pass through a single deep cutting,. or along a single high embankment. Bridges and viaducts across rivers are the only engineering works of special importance that had to be undertaken." In England tunnels, cuttings, embankments and bridges abound and have swelled the total cost.

In America where mountains have been pierced and mighty rivers spanned and every engineering problem known to railway construction has been surmounted, the cost of railways has been only one-half that through the level plains of North Germany.

Cost of French Railways.

French railways whether built by the government or by companies show a capital expenditure more than two and a half times greater than ours. Railway history in France begins with 1840 and Mulhall gives the cost of early construction as follows:

	Cost per Mile.	Ratio.
Land	£ 2,540	8.0
Earthworks	11,430	36.0
Rails, engines, cars	12,700	40.0
Stations, etc.	5,080	16.0
Total	£31,750	100.0

This may be compared with the cost of the Paris and Rouen road as given in the **London Mining Journal**, reprinted in the **American Railroad Journal** (January 30, 1845) as follows:

Law charges, engineering and direction	£ 800
Land and compensation	2,300
Railway works and stations	17,000
Carrying establishment (equipment)	2,400
Total	£22,500

As the line from Paris to Rouen was described as one of "the two most important railways in France" in a contemporaneous technical publication, it does not seem credible that Mulhall's average figures for 1840 can be correct. By 1885 he says the average cost had "diminished" to "exactly £27,000." Since 1895 we have the following official data:

Year.	Miles.	Cost of Construction.	Cost per Mile.
1896	22,649	$3,060,697,600	$135,136
1900	23,701	3,202,901,600	135,138
1904	24,755	3,313,980,000	133,871

The greater cost of French roads compared with German is probably due to the greater density of population and consequent increased expeditures for land damages when they were originally built. These it will be perceived in the case of the Paris and Rouen road amounted to over $11,000 per mile at a time when there were 178 persons per square mile in France to only 151 in Germany. The condition as to density of population has been reversed in late years.

The high cost of railways in Belgium is almost wholly attributable to the combination of density of population with state extravagance either in constructing or acquiring them. Belgium had a population of over 360 to the square mile in 1830 which has risen to over 600 now, or more than double the density of New Jersey.

Cost of Japanese Railways.

Perhaps the most instructive sidelight as to the cost of modern railways is to be obtained by comparison with those of Japan. How absolutely modern is the experience of Japan with railways may be judged from the fact that in 1871 there was not a single mile of line in the empire, which even then had a population of 33,000,000, or more than 200 persons to the square mile. As late as 1880 the railway mileage of Japan was only 121 miles.

The last report of the Director of the Imperial Railway Bureau of Japan states the total mileage open for traffic to March 31, 1906, to be—

Railway Mileage in Japan.

Government railways...	1,532 miles.
Private..	3,251 miles.
Total...	4,783 miles.

His report further shows that the cost of constructing this mileage has been:

	Yen.	Cost per Mile (Dollars).
Government railways.........................	159,918,445	$52,202
Private railways.............................	251,640,590	38,742
Total...................................	411,559,035	$43,056

In a separate table "the average construction cost per mile of railways open for traffic" is given as follows:

	Average Cost per Mile.	Exclusive of Rolling Stock Cost.
Government railways............................	$52,202	$44,201
Private railways................................	38,742	31,339
	$43,056	$35,461

This leaves an average of $7,595 per mile as the cost of rolling stock, the character of which is shown to be as follows:

1,717 locomotives, average weight 45.3 tons.

5,340 passenger cars, average seating capacity 33.7 per car.

27,183 "Goods wagons,' average loading capacity 6.8 tons per wagon.

The passenger carriages are divided into the following classes:

First class...	106
Second class..	528
Third class...	2,989
Composite 1st, 2d or 3d class.........................	349
Composite 2d or 3d class..............................	167
Composite 2d, 3d or brake van........................	411
Miscellaneous...	86
Post or brake van.....................................	704
Total...	5,340

Compared with those of the United States the railways are supplied with the following rolling stock per mile of line:

	Japan. No. per 10 Miles Open.	United States. No. per 10 Miles.
Locomotives..	3.6	2.2
Passenger cars.....................................	12.8	1.8
Freight cars..	16.8	80.0

The difference in number of locomotives per mile against the United States is more than made up by the greater weight of engines on American lines. These average over 63 tons exclusive of tenders to 45.3 tons including tenders for the Japanese roads. The passenger traffic in Japan accounts for almost three-fifths of the railway receipts and for the large number of cheap cars. The capacity of our rolling stock for freight is fully six times greater per mile than that of Japan.

If the cost of rolling stock for Japanese railways was over $7,500 per mile it is a reasonable estimate to say that the rolling stock of American railways has cost $15,000 per mile.

The aggregate capital of the private railway companies of Japan in 1906 was 291,256,800 yen; or $19,808,105 more than their reported cost of construction. That this was in no proper sense an over capitalization is proved by the fact that the Japanese government in its scheme to nationalize the railways of the islands, already passed by the Imperial diet, has fixed the price of the seventeen private roads it proposes to acquire far above the cost of construction, as the following table shows:

Price to be Paid for Japanese Roads.

Road to be Acquired.	Mileage.	Cost of Construction.	Price Fixed for Nationalization.	Ratio Net Earnings to Cost, 1906.
Nippon.................	860	$26,682,021	$65,266,270	15.3
Sanyo..................	406	17,917,923	37,021,490	10.4
Kobu...................	28	1,747,066	4,864,510	*11.2
Kansai..................	280	13,619,200	15,604,030	6.4
Saugu..................	26	930,432	1,886,920	10.8
Sobu...................	73	2,604,331	5,163,240	10.9
Boso...................	39	1,024,596	960,760	5.8
Kyoto..................	22	1,725,099	1,381,735	3.0
Kankaku................	94	3,189,689	3,175,963	5.6
Kokuyetsu..............	86	3,564,973	3,566,980	5.4
Nishinari...............	5	876,564	978,257	5.1
Nanao..................	34	762,407	715,186	4.7
Ganyetsu...............	50	1,293,478	977,949	3.5
Tokushima..............	22	644,703	617,961	4.7
Kyushu.................	446	25,473,758	48,827,300	9.7
Kokaido-Tanko..........	208	5,756,896	14,584,090	12.5
Kokaido................	158	5,239,645	5,462,394	1.6
Totals..............	2,837	$113,052,776	$211,055,035	....

This figures out $74,393 per mile as the purchase price of roads whose original cost of construction was slightly under $40,000.

The Japanese government arrived at its valuation of the several railways by multiplying the average net profits in 1902, 1903 and 1904 by twenty, dividing the product by the cost of construction and multiplying the quotient by the paid up capital. A glance at the last column of the table shows that the value of a line was fixed at approximately the cost of construction where net earnings were 6 per cent. on such cost. Where the roads earned more the price advances until it reaches 150 per cent. for the prosperous Nippon and Kokkaido Colliery lines. "Strategic significance" apparently played some part in the estimate of the value of the last named road.

Twenty times the net earnings of the railways of the United States during the years 1904, 1905 and 1906, including taxes in operating expenses would place their value at $12,811,204.320. Excluding taxes and payments for betterments and improvements from operating expenses would give them a value of $14,505,033,120.

If the Japanese formula were applied to American lines severally as it was to those of Japan, their aggregate estimated value would be still greater.

The development of engineering science as applied to railways and the cheapness of Japanese labor during the period since they were first projected account for their comparatively low cost of construction. The cost of labor in Japan can be judged from the following statement of the average rates for train crews:

Enginemen	22 cents to $1.00 per day.
Firemen	15 cents to .37 per day.
Conductors	12 cents to .42 per day.

In Japan unskilled laborers receive from 10 to 30 cents a day according to the nature of their employment and their efficiency.

The average receipts for freight on the government railways in 1906 was 2.01 sen (1.01 cents) per ton mile against 1.80 sen (0.90 cents) on the private roads, and for passengers 1.43 sen (0.72 cents) per mile on government roads against 1.32 sen (0.66 cents) per mile on the private roads.

Cost in Other Parts of the World.

The low cost of the railways of British India is traceable to minimum expenditures for land and labor; the latter is even cheaper than in Japan, the daily wage of unskilled labor being from 4 to 8 cents. Moreover, 7,318, or over one-quarter of the 27,560 miles of Indian railways are only metre or 3 feet $3\frac{3}{8}$-inch gauge roads and correspondingly cheap in construction.

The variation in the cost of the railways in Australian colonies from $34,730 per mile in Queensland to $62,672 in New South Wales is almost wholly a matter of difference in gauges. Queensland has a standard narrow gauge of 3 feet, 6 inches; South Australia has 507 miles of 5-ft. 3-inch gauge, and 1,238 miles of 3-ft. 6-inch; New South Wales has a standard gauge of 4-ft. $8\frac{1}{2}$-inch, and Victoria has 78 miles of 2-ft. 6-inch gauge and the balance is of broad 5-ft. 3-inch construction.

Compared with those of Queensland and South Australia

the capital cost of $45,826 per mile for the narrow 3-ft. 6-in. gauge government railways of New Zealand appears excessive. And this is emphasized by the fact that 1,562 of the 2,406 miles in the colony is laid with steel or iron rails of 53-lb. to the yard or under.

The advance in the cost per mile of New Zealand railways since 1899 is shown in the following statement:

Cost of New Zealand Railways.

	Cost per Mile. (3-ft. 6-in. Gauge.)
1899	$38,225
1900	38,755
1901	38,546
1902	39,734
1903	41,083
1904	43,717
1905	44,516
1906	45,826

An increase of $7,280 or nearly 19 per cent. in cost of construction per mile in the last five years, without any extraordinary work to account for it, would disturb the financial complacency of any less optimistic organization than the government of New Zealand. Between 1901 and 1906 the gross earnings of New Zealand railways increased over 36 per cent. but the percentage of working expenses to earnings rose from 65.30 to 69 while the percentage of net earnings to capital fell from 3.47 to 3.24.

It is impossible to reconcile such conditions with the ideas of economical railway management which prevail in the United States.

The high cost of the narrow gauge (3-ft. 6-inch) railways of the British South African colonies is due to the combination of government construction and the scarcity and consequent high wages of efficient white labor.

An interesting fact in connection with the capitalization of Canadian railways, which differs materially from their reported cost of construction, is that these two items for the Intercolonial

Railway (the government road) are reported at the same amount, $81,238,728. This is over $54,800 per mile and $1,472 per mile more than the capitalization of the railways of the United States for the same year.

One thing stands out distinct above all others as the conclusion to be drawn from this comparative resume of the cost or capitalization of the railways of the world, and that is that the capitalization of the greatest and most efficient system is less per mile than that of any other except those of relatively insignificant extent and traffic.

VIII
COST OF REPRODUCTION

Thus far we have considered only the cost of the construction and equipment of the railways of the United States as it appears in their general balance sheet as an offset to their capitalization. In this it has been established to a reasonable certainty that their cost has apparently exceeded their net capitalization by approximately $1,328,160,000.

Many students and economists, however, maintain that the true measure of the value of American railways is not in what they have cost, or in their earning power, or what their securities stand for in the open markets of the world, but the sum for which they could be duplicated or reproduced today. If it were possible to secure an appraisement of this so much talked of cost of reproduction by a thoroughly competent, conscientious and impartial tribunal, it would go far to correct the popular impression that American railways are overcapitalized. The difficulty would be to secure appraisers with the requisite capacity, industry and impartiality. With their experience in the past the railways may well look askance upon any commission appointed to probe into their affairs. It is common knowledge that in recent years familiarity with any branch of railway management has been an almost universal disqualification for appointment to any official body charged with the duties contemplated in legislation to regulate railways. It is to the credit of our common citizenship that our railway commissions have in time become as efficient as some of them are. In a matter where it is possible for a United States senator to make a mistake of seven billions in judgment or animus, I care not which, it must be obvious that the appointment of a commission to make an official valuation of the cost of reproducing the railway system of the United States calls for the human wisdom of an Abraham Lincoln and the almost superhuman mental detachment of a George Washington.

Granting that reasonably competent appraisers could be found and were appointed, they would be confronted with a task whose conditions would grow beyond them no matter how fast they worked, just as the demands of American industrial development have outstripped the strained resources of its transportation facilities. Besides taking into consideration the infinite minutiae and staggering aggregate of the business we have been discussing, any such inquiry would have to put a valuation upon the almost priceless advantages of location and terminals of present railway systems separately. These, except as they have been included in transfers of ownership under foreclosure proceedings or in reorganizations, are not represented in the present book cost of the railways. In many instances the terminal rights, facilities and property of existing railway companies are worth as much as their total capitalization.

Then, there are their "intangible assets." In Texas the Tax Commissioner has valued these at $152,827,760 over and above the $188,600,939 valuation placed on their physical property by the Railroad Commission.

In his testimony before the Industrial Commission on Transportation in 1899, Samuel R. Callaway, then president of the New York Central, testified:

"I suppose our property in New York is worth more than the entire capital of the road. In fact, you cannot duplicate it for anything."

Nobody familiar with the New York Central's property in New York City and what it means both to the railway and the people of the United States will doubt the accuracy of Mr. Callaway's statement. The Pennsylvania Railroad is spending over $100,000,000 to secure a terminal by tunnels that will bear any comparison to those obtained by its great rival "for a song" when New York City above 42d street was mostly a picturesque rocky pasture for goats. The original cost of the New York and Harlem Railroad, which included right of way to the heart of the city, seventy years ago was only $2,200,000, or less than $84,000 per mile for its 26 miles of line.

After it had spent months and probably years to fit itself

for the work such a conscientious Commission would find that it could only conclude its endless task by adopting some law of averages, and applying them with such discretion as it might possess. Any attempt to deal with details would be to emulate the unnecessary labor of Sisyphus with an accumulating mass to which his fabled rock would seem a mere pebble. When completed, while the valuation might be labeled "official," it would be no more capable of demonstration than the following estimate made from the best evidence at the command of a single investigator:

COST OF REPRODUCTION OF THE RAILWAYS OF THE UNITED STATES AS OF JUNE 30, 1906.

Cost of construction 214,475 miles single track at $35,000 per mile........	$7,506,625,000
Cost of construction 94,743 miles auxiliary track at $10,000 per mile........	947,430,000
Cost of Equipment..	2,760,000,000
Block Signals, 50,000 miles...	60,000,000
Cost of Right of Way, present location and Terminals.................	3,000,000,000
Real Estate, Shops, Tools and Material..............................	500,000,000
Total...	$14,773,055,000

COST OF CONSTRUCTION.

That the foregoing estimate of $35,000 per mile as the cost of physically constructing the 214,475 miles of single track in the United States is a reasonable one may be judged from the following figures of actual construction by several companies during the past seven years:

EXAMPLES OF CHEAP, TYPICAL AND EXPENSIVE CONSTRUCTION IN THE UNITED STATES SINCE 1899.

LOCATION.	Inexpensive	Typical	Expensive
Eastern Road..	$18,300	$35,000	$132,532
Eastern...		57,892	204,809(d)
Central...		63,500	
Southern..	19,663	60,112	133,533(d)
Southwest...		31,678	
Southwest...	11,345	42,949	66,771
Western...	15,000	28,000	274,000(d)
Northwest...	10,350	23,730	229,480(d)
Average...	$14,931	$42,620	$173,520
Miles represented.......................................	180	510	67

(d) Double track.

This statement yields the following summary:

CLASS	Miles	Aggregate Cost
Inexpensive construction	180	$2,687,580
Typical construction	510	21,736,200
Expensive construction	67	11,625,840
Total	757	$36,049,620
Average per mile		47,622
Less average cost of rigt of way		10,388
Net average cost of construction		$37,234

In the statements for the typical roads included in the above, it appeared that the average outlay for right of way was $6,975 per mile. If this is deducted from the average cost of these roads it leaves a net average cost of $35,645, which is in substantial agreement with the average as derived from the above combination of the three classes of construction. This, it is submitted, justifies adopting $35,000 as the average cost of construction throughout the United States, exclusive of cost of right of way.

Moreover, it should be said that the most expensive piece of construction brought to the writer's notice in his inquiries, averaging $816,800 per mile, was not included in the above summary, because of its exceptional character, involving terminal rights, etc. The cost of getting into any of the larger cities is not included in any of these computations.

In further substantiation of the basis of accepting $35,000 as the basis for estimating the cost of construction in reproducing the railways of the United States, the following composite statement of expenses of typical single track construction derived from reports of three different railways—320 miles represented, is submitted:

Composite Statement of Typical Items.

ITEM	Average cost per mile
Engineering...	$1,291
Station grounds...	....
Real estate...	....
Grading...	15,418
Tunnels...	365
Bridges, trestles and culverts...	7,226
Ties...	2,071
Rails...	3,944
Track fastenings...	737
Frogs and switches...	115
Ballast...	1,490
Track laying and surfacing...	2,723
Fencing right of way...	315
Crossings, cattle guards and signs...	93
Interlocking and signal apparatus...	48
Telegraph lines...	145
Station buildings and fixtures...	801
Shops, engine houses and turn tables...	153
Shop machinery and tools...	25
Water stations...	510
Fuel stations...	240
Electric light and power plants...	31
Miscellaneous structures...	155
Legal expenses...	30
General expenses...	511
Total...	$38,437

In order that the reader may perceive for himself where the difference in cost between expensive and inexpensive construction occurs, the following composite summary has been prepared from two sets of returns from each of the classes included in the general summary above:

Itemized comparative statement of cost of expensive and inexpensive construction derived from the reports of two of each kind:

Cost of Items in Cheap and Expensive Construction.

	Cheap construction, average of 21 miles. Cost per mile.	Expensive construction, average of 37 miles. Cost per mile.
Engineering...	$ 830	$1,468
Right of way and station grounds...		
Real estate...		32
Grading...	4,224	32,702
Tunnels...		1,943
Bridges, trestles and culverts...	3,015	10,001
Ties...	898	2,124
Rails...	2,575	4,418
Track fastenings...	523	758
Frogs and switches...	106	167
Ballast...	385	3,716
Track laying and surfacing...	1,703	3,710
Fencing right of way...	161	550
Crossings, cattle guards and signs...	60	175
Interlocking and signal apparatus...		
Telegraph lines...	120	172
Legal expenses...		26
General expenses...	21	684
Total...	$14,615	$62,646

In the case of one of the expensive examples the way lands and real estate cost $14,666 per mile and in the other $6,087—in neither case was terminal rights involved.

It will not escape notice that in none of these itemized statements is full provision made for interlocking and signal apparatus or many of the other fixtures and structures now regarded as indispensable in the construction of a railway of modern efficiency. In the development of the American railway system such things come later—for few of our railways are completely equipped in these respects before they are opened. Cost of construction is affected very much more by the nature of the country through which the railway runs than the standard of its structures, although these vary greatly. My information shows that the inexpensive construction was in comparatively level localities, with very little of what the engineers call "cross drainage," and consequently a minimum of bridges, trestles and culverts. Typical construction traverses a more or less undulating country, or follows a valley of some river crossed by tributary streams involving frequent, but not heavy cuts and provisions for waterways. It has some rough country requiring cuts or fills which swell the item for grading. An examination of the foregoing statements indicates in the differing cost of the items for grading and bridges why some roads cost only $15,000 a mile and others $35,000 and still others over $100,000. When they get into the hills and mountains with cuts, fills and tunnels, or have to invest in heavy masonry or steel structural work the cost soars into the hundreds of thousands.

The general conclusions from the foregoing statements as to cost of construction is borne out by a series of articles in the Railroad Gazette in the fall of 1906, dealing with the "Unit Cost of Railroad Building." Summarized, its examples of cost, "including preliminary surveys, clearing right of way, roadbed, ties, rails, ballast and side tracks, in shape for operation, but not including real estate, stations, equipment or signals," yield the following data:

EXAMPLES OF COST OF CONSTRUCTION.

SINGLE TRACK.

Miles.	LOCATION.	Year.	Cost per mile.
12.13	Texas	1904	$19,649
9.06	Pennsylvania	1902	26,300
15.77	Pennsylvania	1903	37,014
12.00	West Virginia	1904	40,000
4.10	Ohio	1903	40,700
30.08	Pennsylvania	1901	60,628
10.72	West Virginia	1903	78,000
93.86	Average		$46,527

DOUBLE TRACK.

Miles.	LOCATION.	Year.	Cost per mile.
11.00	New York	1898	$ 50,000
3.60	New York	1903	76,000
51.84	Ohio	1905	100,000
1.57	New York	1899	105,186
8.10	West Virginia	1903	154,000
76.11	miles, Average cost per mile		$97,492
169.97	miles, Average cost per mile		$69,430

In only one instance does the Gazette give in detail the cost of the road—that of the 12.13 miles in Texas. This road follows the dividing ridge between two Texan streams, with no side hill cuts, considerable filling, with few openings and mostly on level ground; the details of cost are as follows:

ITEM.	Cost per mile.
Engineering...	$ 522
Grading...	6,363
Bridges, trestles and culverts...	3,434
Ties...	2,211
Rails...	3,101
Track fastenings...	462
Frogs and switches...	97
Ballast...	2,516
Track laying and surfacing...	784
Crossings, cattle guards and signs...	159
Total...	$19,649

It will be observed that several items of cost necessary to the completion of this piece of road are omitted from the statement, which nevertheless affords an interesting basis for comparison with those previously given.

In the same series of articles the Gazette prints the following data respecting quantities and cost of broken stone ballast per mile of track:

	Cubic yds. per mile.	Cost per cubic yd.	Cost per mile.
Single track...	2,323	$0.904	$2,099.99
Double track...	4,910	.904	4,438.64
Four track...	10,085	.904	9,116.84

This agrees with the average cost of ballast where stone is used in the original returns from which the preceding statements were compiled. The total cost of ballasting the 309,218 miles of track in the United States may be safely estimated at $600,000,000.

In support of the foregoing may be cited the following statement of what it would cost to reproduce the Northern Pacific Railroad from figures filed by that road with the Interstate Commerce Commission in June, 1907:

ESTIMATED COST TO CONSTRUCT THE 5,785 MILES INCLUDED IN THE NORTHERN PACIFIC RAILROAD SYSTEM IN 1907:

	Cost per mile.
Engineering (5,785 miles)	$ 1,500
Grading	12,303
Tunnels	757
Bridges, trestles and culverts	3,517
Ties	2,387
Rails	4,765
Track fastenings	632
Frogs and switches	204
Ballast	1,424
Track laying and surfacing	1,309
Fencing right of way	131
Crossings, cattle guards and signs	50
Signal apparatus	29
Telegraph lines	249
Station buildings and fixtures	434
Shops, round houses and turn tables	686
Machinery and tools	190
Docks and wharves	251
Water stations	340
Fuel stations	110
Warehouses	498
Miscellaneous structures	397
Seattle terminal facilities	425
Ferry equipment	106
Legal expenses	50
General expenses	50
Interest and discount	6,159
Contingencies	2,245
Total	$41,198

As the Northern Pacific has about 1,600 miles of auxiliary track estimated to have cost $16,000,000, the average cost would be reduced to about $38,000 per mile of line, or $3,000 more than is herein estimated, for the entire country.

Cost of the Northern Pacific right of way will be considered elsewhere.

COST OF AUXILIARY TRACK.

With the exception of a few miles, none of the construction included in the compilations from which the average cost of building American railways was deduced covered double or other track. In the cases cited from the Railroad Gazette, one mile of siding was included to every nine miles of single track—the average cost of which however was $46,527 per mile. My estimate of $10,000 per mile for auxiliary track, covering second, third, fourth, yard track and sidings, is based on returns covering over 400 miles, some of which give instances of additional track construction costing as high as $18,000, $21,000 and $23,000 per mile, according as the particular work involved more or less reconstruction of the original main track. Scarcely any of such secondary track work fails to involve some revision of the grades and additional expense on the primary track. One piece of double tracking in the middle west cost $3,350,000, in round numbers, for 335 miles, or $10,000 per mile. Irrespective of all other expenditures incidental to track laying, the following items of everage cost are unavoidable:

Cost of Standard Items in Auxiliary Track.

ITEM.	Cost per mile.
Grading	$1,700
Ties	1,300
Rails (65 lbs. per yard)	3,200
Track fastenings	400
Frogs and switches	40
Ballast	1,400
Track laying	1,800
Total for six items	$9,840

As this list is far from exhaustive, or from furnishing a high average piece of subsidiary track construction, it is safe to estimate the average cost of all descriptions of auxiliary track at $10,000 per mile, or $947,430,000 for the whole railway system of the United States.

Cost of Reproducing Equipment.

From what has been previously written in regard to the present cost of railway equipment, it is only necessary to say here that it could not be reproduced for less than the average price of locomotives, and passenger and freight cars. Briefly stated, the number and cost of railway equipment of June 30, 1906,, was approximately as follows:

Locomotives, 51,672 at $12,000	$ 620,064,000
Passenger cars, 42,262 at $6,000	253,572,000
Freight cars, 1,837,914 at $1,000	1,837,914,000
Work cars, 78,736 at $600	47,241,600
Total cost	$2,758,791,600

That the estimated cost of locomotives is a reasonable one is proved by the following weights and prices of current types of locomotives in 1905 furnished by the Baldwin Locomotive Works company:

	Weight (excluding tender) pounds.	Cost
American type	102,000	$ 9,410
Atlantic type	187,200	15,750
Pacific type	227,000	15,830
Ten Wheel type	156,000	13,690
Consolidation type	192,460	14,500
Average price		$13,836

Moreover, the price of locomotives has advanced considerably since 1905, and will continue to advance so long as the cost of labor and material and the unabated demand for more engine power continues.

As to the cost of passenger cars, their price varies from $4,000

NEW ALL-STEEL POSTAL CAR—UNION PACIFIC.

to $14,000 with the ruling average, including postal and baggage cars, rather over $6,000.

It is pertinent to this discussion to quote the recent decision of Commissioner Lane in a case before the Interstate Commerce Commission involving separate accommodations for white and colored passengers on the Nashville, Chattanooga and St. Louis Railway, where he found that:

"The cost of the car allotted to negroes was in the neighborhood of $8,100, while that of the other passenger coach in defendant's No. 93 train was about $8,800. The expense of the small smoking compartment in the latter accounts for nearly all the difference in cost between the two cars."

The history of the road to which this case relates is worthy of study for the light it sheds on another phase of this subject. The construction of the Western and Atlantic Railroad, now leased to the Nashville, Chattanooga and St. Louis Railway, was begun by the State of Georgia under legislative sanction as far back as 1836, but the last rails from Atlanta to Chattanooga were not laid until 1851. For a period of nearly twenty years, rich in vicissitudes and scandals, the state undertook its operation, and finally, in 1870, leased it to a private com-

INTERIOR OF STEEL POSTAL CAR—UNION PACIFIC.
(See preceding page.)

pany at a rental of $300,000 per year, being 6 per cent. on $5,000,000, or $36,232 per mile, the road was said to have cost. In 1890 the road was again leased to the present lessees for 29 years at $420,012 per annum, all renewals and improvements made by the lessee. By the arrangement the state is receiving 8.4 per cent. on its original investment, or 4.2 per cent. on a present valuation of $10,000,000 or over $72,000 per mile, with no risk through a depletion of the lessee's revenues in consequence of arbitrarily reduced rates. The example is an instructive one as to the increase in the value of railway right of way in Georgia during twenty years, and indicates what it would cost to reproduce such a road today.

The cost of freight cars runs from $600 up to $1,200 and $1,400 for the standard 80,000 pound car. Many of the roads are being equipped with steel cars and high grade refrigerator cars. There are standard prices for different parts of freight cars used in settlements between railways which support these figures. For instance:

Bodies of eight wheel box cars according to length, 32 ft. to 40 ft. or over	$330.00 to	$440.00
Ditto, ventilated, 34 ft. to 40 ft. or over	385.00 to	470.00
Bodies of flat cars 32 ft. to 40 ft. or over	155.00 to	200.00
Bodies of drop bottom gondolas according to capacity	200.00 to	330.00
Bodies of hopper bottom gondolas, according to capacity	220.00 to	440.00
Trucks, 25 to 50 tons capacity, per pair	215.00 to	425.90
Trucks with steel or steel tired wheels, extra per car		112.00
Air brakes	27.50 to	35.00
Steel couplers	8.75 to	9.50

When attached to an underframe varying in cost from $100 to $300, according to material and capacity, these items can be assembled into low and high priced freight cars as follows:

	Low.	High.
Bodies	$155.00	$470.00
Frames	100.00	300.00
Trucks	215.00	425.00
Steel wheels		112.00
Metal bolsters		40.00
Metal center sills		40.00
Air brakes	27.50	35.00
Couplers	8.75	9.50
Total	$506.25	$1,431.50

Freight cars, like other railway equipment, suffer depreciation to the extent of from 15 to 20 per cent. from manufacturer's cost immediately they are put into service, becoming "second hand" in transit from shop to road. Notwithstanding this fact, it was brought out in one of the many recent investigations that in 1902 the Berwind-White Coal Company bought 1,000 cars from the Pennsylvania Railroad at $1,187 per car, and refused to sell them back at the same figure.

It is well within the mark to estimate the cost of reproducing the railway equipment of the United States, as it stood on June 30, 1906, at $2,760,000,000. As it stands today, June 30, 1907, it could not be reproduced for less than $3,000,000,000, for, apart from replacements, it has to be increased at the rate

NEW SIDE OPENING SUBURBAN CAR—ILLINOIS CENTRAL.

of over 10 per cent. a year or it becomes inadequate to the demands of American transportation.

PRESENT VALUE OF RAILWAY RIGHT OF WAY.

A scientific valuation of the right of way and real estate of the railways of the United States is an undertaking beyond the resources of the human mind. Like the estimate of the wealth of the United States by the Census Bureau, it must remain an approximation. Mine, as represented in the table of cost of reproduction of American railways, is $3,000,000,000, or about $14,000 per mile of line. If I had the courage of legitimate deductions from the evidence before me, the average would be $20,000 per mile and the aggregate over $4,400,000,000.

That the right of way is valuable in proportion to density of population is a recognized principle the world over. But the relation varies according to the character of the population and the use to which the property is or may be put. In seeking for a basis by which to value the right of way I have utilized this principle as modified by the actual experience of American railways. Happily, the Census Bureau furnishes data regarding the density of population per square mile and the value of land and improvements per acre throughout the United States. Concrete instances of cost of right of way throughout the United States in recent years warrant the multiplication of the Census valuation by 15 to obtain the price which railways would have to pay for right of way, whether obtained at private sale, as most of it has always been, or by condemnation, as some of it has to be when negotiation fails.

As so much depends on the reasonableness of this factor, let me explain how it is arrived at.

To begin with, the Census Bureau average for the whole United States is universal, whereas, the railways have naturally selected their routes through the most populous and richest territory. The official average is reduced by the low value of real property inaccessible by land or water transportation or

A Priceless Freight Yard in Chicago's Front Yard.

through natural causes; the railway average is augmented by the invariable rule of locating roads in the fertile valleys where possible. The law of gravitation has caused the railways to build as near as could be upon the level, which they only leave to follow where man has made land more valuable by his presence and industry in large numbers. Only when the railway deserts the fields and enters towns and cities is this rule of selecting the most costly route, because it pays, abandoned and the right of way is purchased along the line of the least monetary resistance. Even here in some instances it pays to follow the most expensive routes. Vide the Pennsylvania's improvements in New York City.

But it so happens that a majority of the leading railways of the United States secured their present rights of way in and through cities in days when land was comparatively cheap, and populous centers vied with each other in extending inducements to railways to secure the advantages of rail transportation. The difference between the conditions when the railways began obtaining right of way and today is shown in the table of density of population by states in 1830 and 1906. In the United States at large the density is over four times greater now than then, and outside of the original thirteen states it is ten times greater.

Under all the circumstances it seems that six is a low estimate of the ratio to represent the excess of the value of land traversed by the railways over the average value of land in the United States at large.

On top of this is the difference between the value of the land and what the railway has to pay for it. Here I have accepted the opinion of the Railroad Commission of Wisconsin, which is that the cost of railways "includes the value of the right of way, yards and terminals at two and one-half times the prices of adjacent real estate."

Six times two and one-half, or fifteen, therefore, represents the difference between the value of railway right of way and the average value of land throughout the United States. This applied to the figures as supplied by the Census Bureau and by the Interstate Comerce Commission provides the factors for the following table, which shows the density of population 1830 and 1906; average value of land per acre; average value of a mile of right of way (12 acres) and value of railway right of way in the United States by states and territories:

Density of Population and Value of Right of Way per Mile in the United States.

	Density of population per square mile.		Average value per acre.	Average value, right of way per mile	Total value Railway right of way.
	1830	1906	1904		1905
Alabama	6.0	39	$ 13.61	2,448	11,691,648
Arizona		1	2.15	384	699,264
Arkansas	0.6	27	11.82	2,127	8,899,332
California		11	26.67	4,800	31,092,838
Colorado		6	9.61	1,729	8,694,196
Connecticut	61.4	209	275.66	49,618	50,511,633
Delaware	39.2	99	106.90	19,242	6,446,070
Florida	0.6	11	6.36	1,144	4,108,755
Georgia	8.8	42	14.98	2,696	17,367,632
Idaho		2	2.76	496	727,372
Illinois	2.8	97	152.58	27,464	324,899,120
Indian Territory		17	11.00	1,980	5,223,240
Indiana	9.6	76	76.64	13,795	95,392,425
Iowa		40	70.03	12,605	124,423,955
Kansas		20	21.69	3,904	34,515,264
Kentucky	17.2	58	33.41	6,007	19,740,645
Louisiana	4.7	34	16.84	3,031	12,157,341
Maine	13.4	24	22.04	3,967	8,045,076
Maryland	45.3	128	142.16	25,588	36,693,909
Massachusetts	75.9	379	630.42	113,475	240,454,584
Michigan	0.2	45	54.89	9,880	86,835,320
Minnesota		25	38.31	6,895	55,108,836
Mississippi	2.9	37	9.42	1,695	6,225,876
Missouri	2.1	49	50.78	9,140	73,476,460
Montana		2	3.52	633	2,096,251
Nebraska		14	22.10	3,478	23,203,674
Nevada		04	1.74	313	369,340
New Hampshire	49.9	48	47.17	8,580	10,871,493
New Jersey	43.0	292	395.15	71,127	158,186,443
New Mexico		2	1.97	354	898,303
New York	40.3	173	300.08	54,014	450,260,704
North Carolina	15.2	42	12.81	2,305	9,706,155
North Dakota		7	8.27	1,488	4,812,320
Ohio	23.0	109	129.78	23,360	266,815,240
Oklahoma		15	14.49	2,608	6,846,000
Oregon		5	8.85	1,593	2,888,109
Pennsylvania	30.0	155	229.71	41,347	456,600,442
Rhode Island	89.6	460	766.48	137,966	29,248,792
South Carolina	19.3	48	12.95	2,331	7,365,960
South Dakota		6	7.75	1,395	4,278,465
Tennessee	16.3	52	20.90	3,762	13,396,482
Texas		13	9.26	1,666	19,969,669
Utah		4	4.92	885	1,570,877
Vermont		38	33.38	6,008	6,356,464
Virginia	18.7	49	26.18	4,712	18,617,400
Washington		9	12.78	2,300	7,744,100
West Virginia	18.7	45	23.70	4,266	12,495,114
Wisconsin		41	47.56	8,560	61,726,160
Wyoming		1	2.11	379	473,236
United States	6.4	28	$32.75	$13.33	$2,800,227,984

The District of Columbia has been omitted from this significant table because it has no country area to reduce its urban density to a comparable basis. It is a noteworthy fact, however, that the Census Bureau estimates "the true value of real estate and improvements exclusive of railroads, and telegraph and telephone systems" in the District at $21,620 per acre. A mile of right of way in the District, therefore, would cost $259,560 and the aggregate value of the 31 miles of right of way in Washington, D. C., would be $8,046,360, to say nothing of railway area in yards and terminals.

Lest the reader's credulity should be staggered by such figures as these, he should be informed that there is real estate in Chicago upon which a valuation of over $4,000,000 per acre has been put; that there is one terminal occupying property which, according to the assessed valuation of adjoining property, is worth over $1,000,000 an acre. There are several other terminals occupying land fully as valuable. Only last spring (1907) the Chicago and Northwestern, in connection with other purchases for its proposed passenger depot, paid $50,000 for a piece of property west of the river—that is outside of the business center—80 x 80 feet, or at the rate of nearly $8 per square foot. At the average of 12 acres to the mile of right of way, this would approximate $4,224,000 per mile.

The same company recently bought an irregular lot in the vicinity of its proposed new terminal, containing 28,000 square feet for $365,000 or $13 per square foot, which is at the rate of $572,000 per acre or $6,864,000 per mile of right of way 100 feet wide. This is a trifle less than the price paid this summer for the site of the old Fifth Avenue hotel in New York City.

Another road, the Chicago and Western Indiana, in order to extend its trackage, has recently paid $75,000 for a strip of land at 26th Street, Chicago, two miles from the Postoffice, containing 17,125 square feet. This is equivalent to $4.40 per square foot or $193,600 per acre. Seventeen years ago the "Atchison, Topeka and Santa Fe in Chicago" sold 2.12 miles of terminal right of way in this territory for $8,000,000 cash.

Other railways in Chicago have to pay equally high prices for land. It is not pretended that property so bought is worth the price paid for it. But these purchases illustrate what the railways have to pay when they go into the market, as quietly as they can, to obtain land necessary to make extensions imperatively demanded by the public. The Wisconsin Railroad Commission estimates the holdup to be one and one-half times above the value of the property.

Speaking in round numbers, there are 800 miles of main line and 1,400 miles of auxiliary track within the corporate limits of Chicago. The main line alone represents 9,600 acres, or one-thirteenth of its total area. As the fair value of all real estate in Chicago, exclusive of improvements, is assessed at approximately $1,500,000,000 it is clear that the value of railway right of way would amount to about $115,000,000, or about $144,000 per mile of line. The value of land occupied by other tracks, terminals and yards within the city limits is probably as much more. The aggregate would account for a valuation of nearly $20,000 per mile for all railway right of way in Illinois, leaving the rest of Cook County to account for the balance of $7,464 as the State's quota is the foregoing table.

What is true of Chicago and Illinois is true of every other state containing one or several large cities within its borders.

Let me cite from the Census Bulletin the average value of "real property and improvements" per acre in counties in which cities larger than the national capital are located:

COUNTY	Area square miles.	Land value per acre. 1904.	Land value per capita. 1900.
New York, including King's, New York, Queen's and Richmond.	326	$29,433	$1,507
Cook (Chicago).	993	3,727	985
Philadelphia.	130	24,464	1,215
St. Louis City.	61	16,785	1,020
Suffolk (Boston).	51	37,382	1,775
Baltimore City.	30	24,779	842
Cuyahoga (Cleveland).	472	1,915	850
Erie (Buffalo).	1,040	620	883
San Francisco.	47	20,861	1,435
Hamilton (Cincinnati).	405	1,967	1,196
Allegheny (Pittsburg).	758	2,371	1,181
Orleans (New Orleans).	197	1,327	559
Wayne (Detroit).	626	984	993
Milwaukee.	228	2,871	1,048
District of Columbia, Washington.	60	21,620	2,678

Moreover, these valuations are "exclusive of property held by railroads, street railways," etc. If the value per acre be multiplied by 12, the average number of acres in a mile of right of way, and the product by 2½ to represent the premiums railways have to pay for property, the reader can have some idea of the present cost of railway properties in large American cities.

The general accuracy or understatement of the value of right of way in the table on page 128 is borne out by concrete examples gathered from widely separated sources.

In one case, $998 per mile was paid for right of way through four counties of a western state having an average population of 2.5 per square mile. This is a higher average than the table shows for Arizona with 1 inhabitant per square mile; Idaho with 2; Montana with 2; Nevada with .4; New Mexico with 2; Utah with 4 and Wyoming with 1.

In another case, $1,700 was the average paid per mile for crossing two rural counties of a western state having an average of 24 persons per square mile, and $2,550 for crossing three other counties of the same state having an average of 27 persons per square mile. These were comparatively populous counties where the value of right of way was not affected by the presence of large cities. Bearing this fact in mind, they may be compared with Alabama, with its average of $2,448 valuation per mile; Arkansas with $2,127; Colorado with $1,729; Florida with $1,144; Georgia with $2,696; Indian Territory with $1,980; Mississippi with $1,695; North Carolina with $2,305; North Dakota with $1,488; Oklahoma with $2,608; Oregon with $1,593; South Carolina with $2,331; South Dakota with $1,395; and Texas with $1,666.

In a third case, $18,950 per mile was the average paid for building across a county having a population of 112 to the square mile to the outskirts of a large city, which was excluded from the computation for obvious reasons. Had the road been compelled to build another mile into the city its bill for right of way would have been more than doubled, though spread over the whole length of its line across that particular county.

The average for this right of way is only exceeded by that for Connecticut, Delaware, Illinois, Maryland, Massachusetts, New Jersey, New York, Ohio, Pennsylvania and Rhode Island, in all of which the value of railway right of way is enhanced by the high price of urban property through or into which it runs.

One Chicago road which figured that its "waylands" through the state of Illinois from 1897 to 1907 cost an average of $75 per acre or $1,000 per mile of line was confronted with a very different condition when it faced the necessity for the purchase of a mile only 66 feet wide across a 185 acre tract in the environs of Chicago. Here, while it had to pay only $12,000 for the land it needed, its bill for damage to the remainder of the tract was $18,500 and it had to purchase land for a new street laid out through the tract at as much more per acre as it paid for its own right of way, together with the cost of improving the same. So, that one particular mile of "waylands," 66 feet wide, finally stood on the company's purchase account at $53,050, where the 8 acres it actually bought was valued at only $1,500 an acre. From this it can be imagined what the railways would have to pay for right of way into terminals in any of the great cities of the Union, were they called upon to do so today.

The highest price paid by another Chicago road for right of way during the past ten years was $67,000 per mile. Here again the road was already in possession of the real coign of vantage of terminals in all the cities it reaches.

In proceedings before the New Jersey State Board of Equalization of Taxes it was recently testified that the railroads owned 600 acres of upland and 600 acres of submerged lands on the shore line of Hudson County which chiefly consists of Jersey City. Some of this property was assessed as high as $41,000 per acre, when the average value of all real property in the county according to the Census Bureau was only $11,452. Even at the average estimate, railroad right of way in Jersey City would be worth at least $13,000,000. In 1904 Professor Henry C. Adams estimated the value of the Pennsylvania Railroad ferry property in Jersey City for the Census Bureau at $5,698,000.

In further illustration of this point it may be mentioned that the three terminals of the Atlanta, Birmingham and Atlantic Railroad at Atlanta, Birmingham and Brunswick, which have been secured, will cost approximately $7,500,000.

In fact today the cost of access to the coveted centers of the great cities is so nearly prohibitory that only some such wealthy system as the Pennsylvania has the means and daring to essay it. This prohibitive cost of terminals accounts for the fact that twenty-four roads focussing in Chicago possess only six passenger stations among them. This means that a majority of them gain entrance to the greatest railway center in the world over trackage rights or common ownership. It is impossible to capitalize these trackage rights, but it is evident that they represent a railway asset only second to the actual ownership of the terminals in the proprietary roads.

Some idea, however, of the value of these rights at terminals may be formed from the fact that the New York, New Haven and Hartford Railroad this year paid $798,076 rental to the New York and Harlem road for twelve miles of trackage rights from Woodlawn to the Grand Central Station, under a lease made in perpetuity in 1848. Capitalized at 4 per cent. this represents nearly $20,000,000 or $1,662,000 per mile. When it is considered that the cost of the original New York and Harlem Railroad from the City Hall to White Plains (26 miles) was only $2,200,000 sixty years ago the enormous advance in the value of terminal rights then acquired or donated to the early railways becomes apparent.

A foreclosure sale valuation of $362,694 per mile was recently put on the property of the Wheeling Terminal Railway which owned a bridge and about 10 miles of terminal track at Wheeling, W. Va.

Reverting to the statement of present cost filed by the Northern Pacific Railroad with the Interstate Commerce Commission already referred to, it contained a summary of value of right of way and station grounds at large terminals fully confirming the foregoing estimates and deductions. This summary was as follows:

Value of Right of Way and Stations of Northern Pacific Railroad.

LARGE TERMINALS	Acres.	Total value.
Superior.	982.62	$1,552,020
Duluth.	600.91	5,155,204
Duluth Union Depot.	6.94	420,625
St. Paul.	676.97	9,574,177
Minneapolis.	284.61	5,065,082
Spokane.	422.31	7,240,293
Tacoma.	680.84	12,160,000
Seattle.	461.03	30,167,000
Butte.	233.76	2,000,000
Everett.	124.68	374,040
Bellingham.	67.86	339,300
South Bend.	35.63	249,419
Aberdeen and Hauquaim.	69.83	698,300
Total large terminals.	4,637.99	$75,000,501
Other right of way and station grounds	152,185.00	31,889,589
Total.	$156,822.99	$106,890,090
Value per acre.		$681
Acres per mile of line.		27.11
Value per mile of line.		$18,477

This statement indicates how far within the mark is my estimate of $14,000 as the average value of railway right of way per mile in the United States based on the assumption that "waylands" 100 feet wide would cover not only main line but land for auxiliary tracks, sidings, yard tracks and station grounds. Applied to the whole country the averages for the Northern Pacific would support an estimate of $20,000 per mile, or more than $4,400,000,000 as the present value of the right of way and station grounds of the railways of the United States.

Touching the justice of including the present value of their possessions in any estimate of the cost of reproducing the railways of the United States the Railroad Commission of Wisconsin, owing its appointment to Senator La Follette, has admitted that:

"It can perhaps be said that the owners of railroad property are entitled to any increase in the value of their property that may accrue from the progress of the territory in which it lies, and that they have as much right to the natural increments in the physical value of their property as the owners of any other property.'"

If the Commission had been entirely just it would have gone further and said there was no "natural increment" about the increase in the value of railway property to which they have not contributed by far the greater share. Without the railways built in Wisconsin since 1850 the increase of the wealth of Senator La Follette's state from $42,056,595 in that year to $2,838,678,239, or over 6,650 per cent. would have been as impossible as, looking backwards, it seems incredible.

There has been no "unearned increment" about the advance in the value of the physical property of the railways.

It is needless in such a work as this to more than remind the reader that the increase in land values has not been confined to the cities, but has its counterpart throughout the country. One example will suffice to illustrate this point. The late William (Lord) Scully, of absentee landlord fame, bought farm lands in Illinois in 1851 from the government at $1.25 per acre which he rented in 1900 at $3 per acre per annum.

IX

COMMERCIAL AND MARKET VALUATION

In 1905 the Statistician of the Interstate Commerce Commission, Professor Henry C. Adams, as the authorized agent of the Census Bureau, reported what has been currently known as the "Commercial Valuation of Railway Operating Property in the United States." This report, which was made as "one step in the determination of the wealth of the nation," placed the value of railway operating property, computed for the year 1904, at

$$\$11,244,852,000.$$

This valuation was arrived at by capitalizing what was called "their true net earnings" at a rate arrived at by an elaborated formula based on "the market price of their securities."

In his computation for the Census Bureau, Professor Adams very wisely freed himself from all the "entangling alliances" and duplications arising from including "non-operating" with operating railways in his statistical work for the Interstate Commerce Commission. By adopting the "operating railway systems as the units of appraisal," as expressed by the Director of the Census, he was enabled to arrive at a result the value of which depends solely on the acceptance of two elusive factors, viz., "true net earnings," and the rate determined on for their capitalization.

Professor Adams arrived at the former by subtracting reported operating expenses, less such sums as were spent for permanent improvements and charged to operating expenses, from gross earnings from operation. From the remainder he subtracted the amount of taxes paid. The final balance was accepted as the true profit from operation.

This afforded a very simple formula, but an attempt was made to equalize the result by taking the average of profits from operation of certain roads for five years, and of others for three, and estimating the value of others on mileage, gross earnings, operating expenses, etc.

With the aid of Professor B. H. Meyer, of the Railroad Commission of Wisconsin, Professor Adams arrived at 4.256 per cent. as the exact rate for the capitalization of the "true net earnings" as previously ascertained.

By supplementing these methods with others to meet isolated cases, Professor Adams and his assistants compiled the following statement of the commercial value of the railways of the United States for the year 1904 (Vide Census Bulletin 21, page 9):

	Valuation.	Per cent of total.
Capitalization of net earnings:		
(a) Rate based on market quotations	$10,385,264,000	92.35
(b) Rate based on formulae	705,418,000	6.27
Operated mileage	87,235,000	.78
Gross earnings	11,288,000	.10
Operating expenses	2,828,000	.03
Cost of construction, etc	5,755,000	.05
Some or all of debt	22,871,000	.20
Appraisal for taxation	1,816,000	.02
Income from lease	22,318,000	.20
Actual sale of entire property	59,000	
Total	$11,244,852,000	100.00

As this valuation rests on "the capitalization of the average net earnings for a period of five years preceding June 30, 1904," it is obviously a valuation for 1901-2 rather than for 1904. As the net earnings of the railways from operation in 1904 were $42,585,342 greater than the average for the five year period preceding, it is equally obvious that using the rate determined on, viz., 4.256 per cent., the capitalized value of the railways would have been almost exactly $1,000,000,000 more than as estimated on the period named.

Now if the method of valuation of Professors Adams and Meyer be applied to the earnings for the year ending June 30, 1905, and estimating the cost of permanent improvements charged to operating expense, we obtain the following:

Commercial Value, 1905.

Gross earnings from operation..................		$2,082,482,406
Expenses of operation......................	$1,390,602,152	
Less permanent improvements charged to operating expense...................	20,000,000	1,370,602,152
Income from operation................		$ 711,880,254
Less taxes.................................		63,474,679
"True net earnings"..........................		$ 648,405,575
Capitalized at 4.256% = ...		$15,235,093,400

If the same methods were applied to the railway income for the year ending June 30, 1906, the results would be still more surprising, as the following statement shows:

Commercial Value, 1906.

Gross earnings from operation..................		$2,325,765,167
Expenses of operation......................	$1,536,877,271	
Less permanent improvements charged to operating expense	20,000,000	1,516,877,271
Income from operation................		$808,887,896
Less taxes.................................		74,785,615
"True net earnings".........................		$734,101,281
Capitalized at 4.256% = ...		$17,248,620,000

If the formula adopted by Professors Adams and Meyer and accepted by the Census Bureau is entitled to credit, the commercial value of the railways of the United States on June 30, 1906, was approximately $17,248,620,000.

Even if the rate 4.256 be applied to the average "true net earnings" of the last period of five years, 1902 to 1906, inclusive, the commercial value according to the official formula would be approximately $14,840,000,000. This of course is a mean commercial value for the term of years and not at the end of the term when the "true net earnings" were fully $232,000,000 more than at the beginning.

When the returns for 1907 are all in it will be found that the commercial value of the railways of the United States according to the formula adopted by the Census Bureau is over $19,000,000,000.

But it must be obvious to the most casual student that this

so-called commercial valuation of the railways is merely a capitalization of the earning capacity of the railways, which must rise and fall with the prosperity of the public they serve. In no way does it go to establish "the value of the transportation plant employed in the service of that public."

The sole purpose for which a separate valuation of the physical property of the railways is sought by the Interstate Commerce Commission is that it may be used in "determining the reasonableness or unreasonableness of rates." As this commercial valuation depends absolutely on income arising from the rates, even Professor Adams admits "that such a valuation cannot be used" for that purpose.

That it could be and would be used as a basis of values in case the Government were considering the purchase of railways is indicated by the procedure adopted in Germany and Japan.

Market Value of the Railways.

Little need be said of the value of the railways of the United States as reflected in daily market quotations. These are affected by influences so entirely independent of the value of the railways, and often so independent even of their income earning capacity, as to be practically worthless as a measure of value.

In 1900 when the net capital of the railways of the United States was $9,547,984,611, the Interstate Commerce Commission made a report of their market value to the Senate as follows:

Ascertainable market value...	$8,351,103,523
Not ascertainable (par value)...	812,066,859
Total..	$9,163,170,382

In short, in 1900 the market value of railway securities was 96 per cent. of their net capitalization. In 1905 their net capitalization had risen to $11,167,105,992 and on a basis of 96 per cent. their market value would have been approximately $10,720,420,000.

But between 1900 and 1905 the quoted market value of railway securities had advanced an average of 20 per cent, making their market value two years ago approximately $12,864,500,000.

In 1906 there was a further increase both in the capitalization and market value of railway securities, so by the end of last year it is safe to estimate the latter at $13,000,000,000.

Then came the great decline of last March which in the course of a few weeks demonstrated the utter worthlessness of market prices as a measure of the values of railway property. With every railway in the country in better physical condition than ever before in its history; with their facilities taxed to the utmost by unprecedented traffic; with gross earnings surpassing all records and net earnings showing a healthy increase; with the business of the republic betraying no signs of a recession—in the face of the most favorable conditions—so far as railway earnings were concerned—the market value of their securities in six months showed a shrinkage on June 30, 1907, of no less than $2,000,000,000.

That this decline of two billions is not a mere estimate is proved by the fact that the shares of 54 companies having an aggregate capital stock of $4,481,400,000 showed an actual shrinkage of $1,361,505,000 in market value in the first six months of 1907. This is equivalent to a decline of over 30 per cent. If the remainder of the capital stock suffered a like decline it would amount to no less than $1,966,000,000 for all the railways. As there was a shrinkage of over 6 per cent. in the market values of railway bonds aggregating at least $360,000,000, the total decline in the market values of railway securities must have been fully $2,300,000,000.

Any measure of values liable to a shrinkage of from 15 to 20 per cent. in the face of an increase in the physical, commercial, taxable and earning value of the railways must be rejected as valueless in ascertaining their true valuation.

Furthermore, in 1900 when the Interstate Commerce Commission reported its estimate of $9,163,170,382 as the market value of all the railways to the United States Senate, it reported the net interest and dividends paid by the railways as follows:

Net interest on funded debt	$242,998,285
Interest on current liabilities	4,912,892
Net dividends	118,624,409
Total	$366,535,586

This sum is an inappreciable shade over 4 per cent. on the market value as reported by the Commission.

In 1905 and 1906 the railways reported the payment of interest and dividends under the same heads as follows:

	1905 (Full Returns).	1906 (94% Returns).
Net interest on debt	$294,803,884	$252,572,777
Interest on current liabilities	11,451,400	13,819,287
Net dividends	188,175,151	221,507,203
Total	$494,430,435	$487,899,267

Capitalized at 4 per cent., the rate fixed in the Commission's report in 1900 the net interest and dividends paid in 1905 would justify a market valuation for that year of approximately $12,360,000,000 and in 1906 for 94 per cent. of the roads of $12,197,000,000.

But as market values as revealed in daily stock quotations are influenced as much by the price of money in London as by the earnings or true value of American railways such estimates as these possess little more than a speculative interest, except as they afford cumulative testimony to the point that American railways are not over capitalized.

If the prevailing rate of interest were ever to go to 8 per cent., where it was when many of our railways were projected, the market value of American railways would shrink nearly 50 per cent., but that would not affect their cost, true value, or capitalization. It would only make it more difficult for them to provide adequate service for the American people.

The difficulty with the railways today, then, is not over-capitalization, but where to get more capital to enable them to keep pace with the business demands made upon them. With Boston, New York City and New York State failing to float 4 per cent. bonds at par, and the railways forbidden to go near the "water," the prospect for necessary improvements and extensions is very dry indeed.

X

VALUATION AS ESTABLISHED BY TAXATION

In the year 1904 the "estimated true value of all property" in the United States as set forth by the Director of the Census was

$107,104,192,410.

In this total was included for "Railroads and their Equipment" exclusive of "railroads which in certain states are classed as real property" the sum of

$11,244,752,000,

being just $100,000 short of the commercial value of railway operating property compiled for the Census Bureau by Professor Henry C. Adams, the statistician of the Interstate Commerce Commission.

For 1904 the Census Bureau found that the "assessed valuation of all property (real and personal) subject to ad valorem taxation" in the United States was $38,963,381,120, or only 36.4 per cent. of the estimated true value of all property in the country as given above. (See diagram next page.)

If the railway property included in the major total had been assessed on the same basis as all property, its assessed valuation, exclusive of that classed as real property in certain states, would have been $4,095,089,728.

Now it so happens that Professor Adams in submitting his report on the commercial value of the railways for the Census Bureau in 1904 presented a table which he called "A comparison between the Actual Commercial Value of Railway property devoted to transportation and the latest reported values of railway property assessed for purposes of taxation in various states and territories." For some unexplained reason no less than seven states, including three of the most important, were omitted entirely from the table. Incomplete as it was this table showed that the railway property assessed for taxation amounted

Diagram and Table.

Estimated True Value of All Property, and Assessed Valuation of Portion Subject to Ad Valorem Taxation for Each State and Territory, 1904; *vide* "Wealth, Debt and Taxation," Official Reports of the Census Office, 1907, pages 28 and 41.

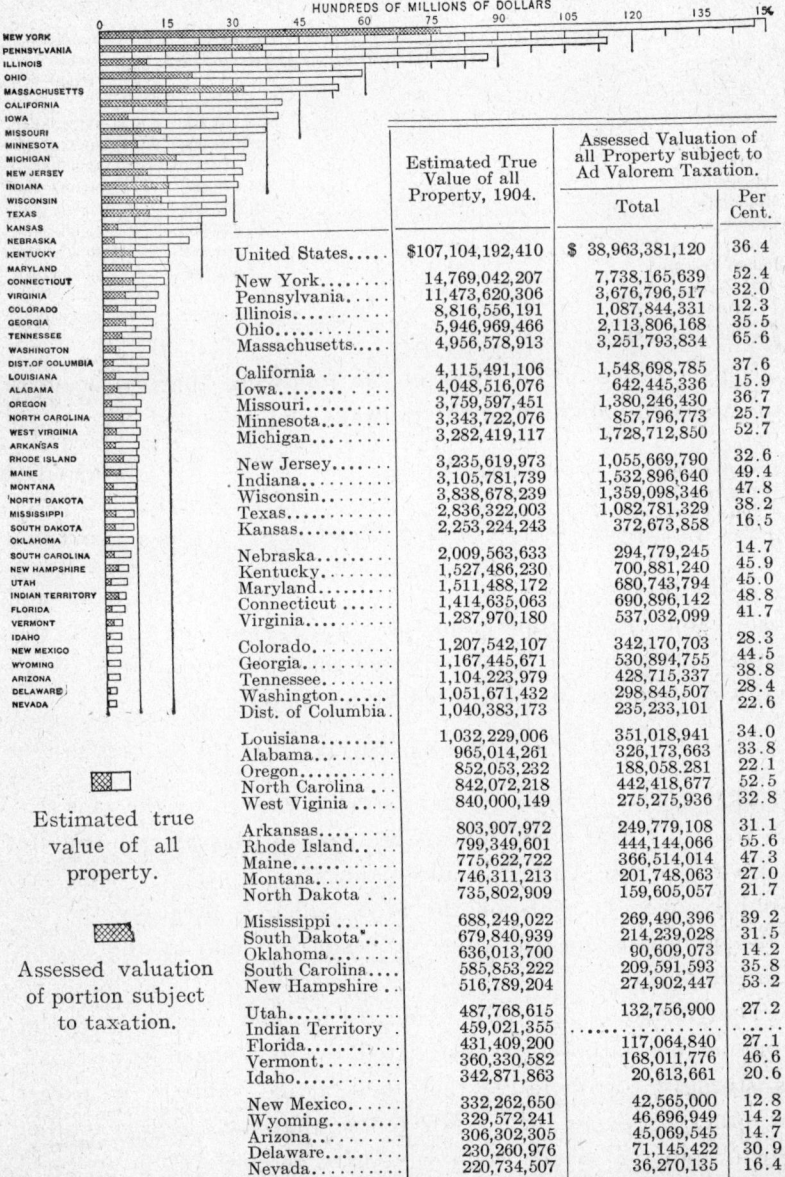

■□ Estimated true value of all property.

▨ Assessed valuation of portion subject to taxation.

	Estimated True Value of all Property, 1904.	Assessed Valuation of all Property subject to Ad Valorem Taxation.	
		Total	Per Cent.
United States	$107,104,192,410	$ 38,963,381,120	36.4
New York	14,769,042,207	7,738,165,639	52.4
Pennsylvania	11,473,620,306	3,676,796,517	32.0
Illinois	8,816,556,191	1,087,844,331	12.3
Ohio	5,946,969,466	2,113,806,168	35.5
Massachusetts	4,956,578,913	3,251,793,834	65.6
California	4,115,491,106	1,548,698,785	37.6
Iowa	4,048,516,076	642,445,336	15.9
Missouri	3,759,597,451	1,380,246,430	36.7
Minnesota	3,343,722,076	857,796,773	25.7
Michigan	3,282,419,117	1,728,712,850	52.7
New Jersey	3,235,619,973	1,055,669,790	32.6
Indiana	3,105,781,739	1,532,896,640	49.4
Wisconsin	3,838,678,239	1,359,098,346	47.8
Texas	2,836,322,003	1,082,781,329	38.2
Kansas	2,253,224,243	372,673,858	16.5
Nebraska	2,009,563,633	294,779,245	14.7
Kentucky	1,527,486,230	700,881,240	45.9
Maryland	1,511,488,172	680,743,794	45.0
Connecticut	1,414,635,063	690,896,142	48.8
Virginia	1,287,970,180	537,032,099	41.7
Colorado	1,207,542,107	342,170,703	28.3
Georgia	1,167,445,671	530,894,755	44.5
Tennessee	1,104,223,979	428,715,337	38.8
Washington	1,051,671,432	298,845,507	28.4
Dist. of Columbia	1,040,383,173	235,233,101	22.6
Louisiana	1,032,229,006	351,018,941	34.0
Alabama	965,014,261	326,173,663	33.8
Oregon	852,053,232	188,058.281	22.1
North Carolina	842,072,218	442,418,677	52.5
West Viginia	840,000,149	275,275,936	32.8
Arkansas	803,907,972	249,779,108	31.1
Rhode Island	799,349,601	444,144,066	55.6
Maine	775,622,722	366,514,014	47.3
Montana	746,311,213	201,748,063	27.0
North Dakota	735,802,909	159,605,057	21.7
Mississippi	688,249,022	269,490,396	39.2
South Dakota	679,840,939	214,239,028	31.5
Oklahoma	636,013,700	90,609,073	14.2
South Carolina	585,853,222	209,591,593	35.8
New Hampshire	516,789,204	274,902,447	53.2
Utah	487,768,615	132,756,900	27.2
Indian Territory	459,021,355		
Florida	431,409,200	117,064,840	27.1
Vermont	360,330,582	168,011,776	46.6
Idaho	342,871,863	20,613,661	20.6
New Mexico	332,262,650	42,565,000	12.8
Wyoming	329,572,241	46,696,949	14.2
Arizona	306,302,305	45,069,545	14.7
Delaware	230,260,976	71,145,422	30.9
Nevada	220,734,507	36,270,135	16.4

to $3,027,144,820. It has been computed from such figures as are available that the assessed values of the railway property in the omitted states compared with their Commercial Value as found by Professor Adams were as follows:

	Estimated Assessed Value 1904.	Commercial Value 1904.
Delaware	$10,153,500	$ 17,285,000
Maine	49,038,900	80,146,000
Maryland	57,919,200	132,342,000
Massachusetts	307,076,600	250,052,000
Minnesota	301,567,600	466,734,000
Oregon	40,336,700	75,661,000
Pennsylvania	517,101,312	1,420,608,000
Indian Territory	6,662,900	79,405,000
Total	$1,289,856,712	$2,522,233,000

This enables us to arrive at the following approximation of the assessed valuation of the railways of the United States:

Assessed valuation as found by Professor Adams	$3,027,144,820
Assessed value for States omitted	1,289,856,712
	$4,317,001,532

If the proportion of 36.4 per cent. between assessed value and true value of all property in the United States be correct, this table approaches a demonstration that the true value of all railway property of the United States in 1904 was

$11,841,589,000.

That this estimate is not far astray is proved by the fact that in 1905, the year when taxes were paid on this assessment, the railways of the United States paid $63,324,551 in taxes, or slightly over 53 cents on the $100, which is precisely the tax rate applied to the true value in Texas as found by the Census Bureau.

That it should approach so nearly to their value in 1904 for commercial purposes, as estimated by the official statistician, is strongly corroborative that their actual value is in excess of either aggregate. It is safe to say that there is not another great industry in the country, where the return on invested capital is so small, which pays such a large proportion of its net earnings in taxes, amounting in the days of its greatest prosperity to over 12 per cent.

Moreover these figures of value of railway property assessed for the purposes of taxation are exclusive of the almost priceless railroad property assessed in New York and New Jersey as real estate. As the New York Central alone in 1906 paid $2,924,593 for taxes on real estate out of a total of $4,126,984, it is evident that the assessed value of railway real estate in New York must have been at least $300,000,000 and last year's railway taxes in New Jersey show that railway real estate in that state must have had an assessed value of over $75,000,000. As the assessed value of all property in New York is 52.4 per cent. of the true value and in New Jersey 32.6 per cent., these two items alone would add over $800,000,000 to the value of railway property as established on the basis of taxable values in the United States, making an aggregate total of

$$\$12,641,589,000.$$

In order that the student may appreciate the varied conditions as to taxation which confront the railways in the various states of the Union, the following table presents the facts as to their mileage, assessed value for taxation, total taxes paid and per mile in the several states from the latest official returns, except as noted, where they were computed:

Railway Assessment and Taxes.

	Mileage 1905.	Assessed for taxation 1904.	Taxes paid 1905.	Per cent of tax on assessed value.	Tax rate per $100 of estimated true value.
Alabama	4,776	$53,926,026	$833,121	1.544	$0.56
Arkansas	4,183	34,709,623	789,442	2.274	0.63
California	6,477	92,378,550	1,919,125	2.077	0.74
Colorado	5,027	49,492,135	1,374,077	2.776	1.00
Connecticut	1,018	120,493,648	1,281,751	1.063	0.61
Delaware	335	10,153,500	101,535	1.000	0.60
Florida	3,590	21,817,478	469,938	2.154	0.68
Georgia	6,442	63,105,810	831,436	1.317	0.78
Idaho	1,465	10,115,378	375,678	3.713	0.61
Illinois	11,830	425,709,055	5,186,887	1.218	0.67
Indiana	6,915	165,863,367	3,096,288	1.866	0.98
Iowa	9,871	57,535,160	2,089,289	3.631	0.61
Kansas	8,841	60,093,534	2,398,209	3.997	0.71
Kentucky	3,286	77,658,040	1,180,298	1.519	0.72
Louisiana	4,011	29,044,195	795,874	2.740	0.92
Maine	2,028	49,038,900	490,389	1.000	0.94
Maryland	1,434	57,919,200	579,192	1.000	0.76
Massachusetts	2,119	307,076,600	3,070,766	1.000	1.06
Michigan	8,789	196,795,000	2,680,851	1.362	0.79
Minnesota	7,992	301,567,600	2,189,953	.726	0.61
Mississippi	3,672	29,847,640	648,417	2.226	0.67
Missouri	8,039	97,916,869	1,594,094	1.628	0.62
Montana	3,309	36,759,827	765,322	2.081	0.60
Nebraska	5,833	46,082,853	1,296,686	2.813	0.71
Nevada	1,180	13,778,049	282,697	2.051	0.30
New Hampshire	1,267	22,625,000	395,328	1.746	0.84
New Jersey	2,224	231,655,525	1,852,786	.799	0.70
New York	8,336	229,582,064	5,066,316	2.206	0.97
North Carolina	4,210	69,480,974	642,466	.924	0.52
North Dakota	3,233	22,160,304	805,756	3.636	0.66
Ohio	9,259	133,858,945	4,297,601	3.210	0.87
Oregon	1,813	40,336,700	403,367	1.000	0.66
Pennsylvania	11,043	517,101,312	3,586,872	.694	0.56
Rhode Island	212	15,832,003	222,233	1.403	0.81
South Carolina	3,160	29,467,716	495,750	1.682	0.70
South Dakota	3,067	14,354,930	325,306	2.266	0.70
Tennessee	3,561	58,536,566	832,869	1.422	0.74
Texas	11,983	95,209,785	1,274,694	1.338	0.53
Utah	1,774	20,682,461	461,885	1.991	0.63
Vermont	1,058	27,344,020	156,850	.573	0.55
Virginia	3,950	63,269,623	1,219,316	1.927	0.58
Washington	3,367	26,066,949	826,722	3.171	0.98
West Virginia	2,929	28,771,358	599,804	1.751	0.73
Wisconsin	7,211	218,024,900	2,262,303	1.037	0.78
Wyoming	1,247	7,498,232	200,491	2.673	0.35
Arizona	1,821	6,667,349	230,792	3.476	0.57
District of Columbia	32	2,486,024	41,966	1.285	0.34
Indian Territory	2,638	6,662,900	33,329	.500	0.07
New Mexico	2,534	8,511,538	278,618	3.273	0.47
Oklahoma	2,625	11,936,317	453,816	3.802	0.56
United States	217,017	$4,317,001,532	$63,324,551	1.467	$0.74
Assessed as real estate in New York		300,000,000			
Assessed as real estate in New Jersey		75,000,000			
Total assessed value		$4,692,001,532			

As all property in the United States is assessed on an average of 36.4 per cent. of its estimated true value (Table 16, Census Report, Wealth, Debt and Taxation 1907) this assessed value of $4,692,001,532 represents an estimated true value of approximately

$$\$12,890,000,000.$$

The variation of $248,411,000 between this result and that arrived at on page 147 is due to the disturbance of the ratio between the assessed value and the "estimated true value" by the introduction of estimates for the states omitted in the Census table of assessed values and the estimates of real estate values excluded from the assessed values in New York and New Jersey.

Whichever figure is accepted establishes the fact, that on the basis of assessed valuations and taxes compared with their relation to the official estimated true value of all property in the United States, the value of American railways for taxation purposes is greater than their net capitalization of

$$\$11,671,940,649.$$

An analysis of the last two columns in the above table demonstrates that the rate paid by the railways on the assessed value of their property is from 1 to 7 times greater than the tax rate paid per $100 of estimated true value of all property in the United States. In the country at large it is twice as great.

Texas affords a striking illustration of the difference between the tax levied on railways and the rate paid on general property. Although the taxes levied on the railways of Texas were only 1.338 per cent. on their assessed value, this was 2.53 times more than the average rate levied on private property throughout the state. In 1906 the Texas railways were assessed at $10,907 per mile for purposes of taxation and the taxes actually paid by them amounted to $1,594,825 or 1.212 on their assessed value which is 2.3 times more than the rate levied on the true value of all property in Texas. This would make it appear that their true value for taxation purposes was $25,086 per mile, or $8,555 more than the valuation put on them by the State Railroad Commission.

According to the assessors, the value of Texas railways increased $2,456 per mile between 1905 and 1906, while the Commission could only find that their value had increased $11 per mile, which shows the difference whether the appraiser is seeking to increase the revenues of the state or for excuse to reduce the revenues of the railways.

In passing, it is worthy of note that while the net capitalization of the railways of the United States has increased only 28.7 per cent. during the last ten years **their taxes have increased over 87 per cent.**

The railways of Minnesota, according to the State Commission, paid $3,015,676 taxes in 1905 against $1,911,707 in 1904.

Where the railways of New Jersey are credited in the above table with having paid only $1,852,786 taxes in 1904, the total tax upon them for state uses in 1906 was $3,509,371.

With these examples of what consideration the railways are receiving at the hands of taxing bodies, I leave this phase of the subject.

XII

RECEIVERSHIPS AND THE RAILWAYS

Among the many things laid at the door of alleged over-capitalization of American railways are the periodic succession of receiverships that have seared their history with the brand of financial tribulation. Even the fairest writers on railway economics have not escaped this pitfall dug by political agitators for the delusion of the unwary. Professor Emory R. Johnson in his "American Railway Transportation," one of the ablest and most instructive of recent works on the subject, falls into the popular error, when he says, "The large number of railroad receiverships in the United States has been the result of several causes, of which the first and most potent has been over-capitalization."

As a matter of fact, there is not the slightest evidence to sustain such a sweeping assertion. That over-capitalization has in a few flagrant cases contributed to forcing companies into the hands of receivers may be admitted. But the four "most potent" causes of railroad receiverships in the United States have been faulty location, over-construction, over-competition and successive business depressions.

This is not the assertion of a theory but of conditions susceptible of proof. Where roads have been originally located correctly with good judgment where needed, and where the immediate prospects or far-seeing prescience justified large expenditures, receiverships have been the rare exceptions.

In discussing this phase of the subject one salient fact should never be lost sight of—only the capitalization represented by bonds has any bearing on the question of receivership. It is only when the security of the bondholder is imperilled that the protection of the courts is invoked.

The Halt of 1837.

The first financial storm the railways had to meet was that of 1837, when the initial cost of construction of the early roads had imposed a heavy burden upon the capital and industry of the country. The result was, as we read in Poor's Manual, that in many of the states, particularly in the Western and Southern, large sums were expended upon lines which were wholly abandoned. Charters granted and work begun in 1834-1836 were held in abeyance, not to be revived or resumed until along in the early forties, after the effect of the revulsion began to wear off.

The Galena and Chicago Union, the forerunner of the Chicago and Northwestern, affords an illustration of what happened to the railways of the United States at that time. On January 10, 1836, it received a special charter from the legislature of Illinois to build a railroad out into the prairie country toward the Mississippi. An amended charter was granted in 1837, under which a short preliminary survey was made and 940 acres of wood land nine miles west of Chicago was secured as a source of fuel supply. "Then," says the historian, "the financial 'panic' beginning in the summer of 1837 put a stop to this and many other railroad projects, not only in Illinois but all over the United States." The actual construction of the Galena and Chicago Union was not resumed until 1847.

It was the financial upheaval of 1837 that induced the state of Michigan to take over the construction of the Detroit and St. Joseph railroad chartered in 1836 (the original Michigan Central) and the Erie and Kalamazoo Railroad chartered in 1833 (now a part of the Lake Shore and Michigan Southern Railway). The former company was capitalized at $2,000,000, but no work had been done upon it when the state of Michigan appointed commissioners to complete the construction. Appropriations were made for this purpose in 1838, 1839, 1843 and 1844, and in 1846 the road was completed 144 miles to Kalamazoo.

A report to the legislature when work had proceeded 110

miles to Marshall gives the following details respecting this piece of forced government ownership:

COST OF MICHIGAN CENTRAL AND MICHIGAN SOUTHERN
TO DECEMBER 31, 1844.

Central (110 miles completed)		$1,842,308
Southern (initial point at Monroe)		936,295
		$2,778,603
10% added for interest during construction and other incidental expenses		277,860
Palmyra and Jackson Railroad, cost including interest		30,000
Locomotives and cars on Central Railroad	$110,000	
Ditto on Southern Railroad	51,000	161,000
Total		$3,257,963

Governor Barry reported in favor of selling these works, which were subsequently sold to Boston capitalists for $2,000,000 for the Central and $500,000 for the Southern. They were paid for in state bonds which the shrewd New Englanders had bought at 70 cents on the dollar, thereby obtaining for $1,750,000 property which had cost at least $3,500,000. All told, Michigan spent $4,500,000 and 305,000 acres of public land on her railroads, and they were worth the expenditure, although Boston financiers bought them in at what would now be called "bargain counter" prices. The purchasers had to go into the markets to raise additional funds for their rehabilitation, completion, extension and equipment.

THE PANIC OF 1857.

After the country recovered from the effects of the "financial catastrophe" of 1837, the extension of railways into every quarter of the West proceeded with unprecedented rapidity until checked temporarily by another panic; when, again we read in the histories, "A great financial revulsion came in 1857 and at once put a stop to further construction of this and many other lines of railroad and this company became bankrupt." The road here referred to was the Chicago, St. Paul & Fond du Lac Railroad, all of whose property, franchises and rights were purchased at foreclosure sale by the newly organized Chicago and Northwestern Railway for $10,849,938 in stocks and bonds of the purchasing company.

A like process went on all over the country. The financially sound companies—i. e., those which had not been over-built into unproductive territory—buying in the property of the bankrupt companies below cost of construction, but almost never below the face of the funded debt.

The Receiverships of 1873.

Scarcely had the railways recovered from the business depression of 1857, when the civil war brought nearly all industrial progress to a standstill and by its legacy of inflated currency prepared the way for the financial convulsion of 1873. Between 1860 and 1865 only 3,303 miles of railway were built in the United States, but with the return of peace in the latter year construction was resumed with feverish activity. The mileage jumped from 35,085 miles in 1865 to 70,651 in 1873—that is, it more than doubled in eight years.

In 1860 there were 1026 inhabitants to each mile of railway; in 1870 the proportion was only 730, and by 1873 it had fallen to 590 per mile of road. As experience at that stage in the development of railway economies had demonstrated that "to enable railroads to be operated at a profit a population of at least 850 to a mile of railroad is necessary in this country" (Poor's Manual 1877-1878), the over building of railways had passed below the margin of safety in 1870, and was far below it in 1873, when the country entered upon that period of depression from which it did not emerge until specie payment was resumed and all business was once more placed on a sound money basis.

No fine-drawn theory is needed to explain the railway receiverships of 1874 to 1877. It is told in unmistakable language in the following table of earnings—gross and per mile.

	Gross Earnings.	Per Mile.
1872	$465,241,055	$8,116
1873	526,419,935	7,933
1874	520,466,016	7,513
1875	503,065,505	7,011
1876	495,257,959	6,765
1877	472,909,272	6,381

The startling decrease in gross earnings per mile between 1872 and 1877 shows the combined effect of the business depression and over-construction. In spite of a slight increase in gross earnings, it will be perceived that there was a decrease of more than 20 per cent. in earnings per mile. The large receipts per mile previous to 1871 had furnished the stimulus for the over-construction which swept scores of railways into bankruptcy during the business stagnation which waited on the restoration of our currency to a healthy basis.

In passing, it is worthy of note that twenty years had to elapse before (in 1901) the gross receipts of the railways of the United States reached the level per mile from which they fell as shown in the foregoing table.

An examination of the reports of the principal systems which went into the hands of receivers in 1874 discloses the fact that their difficulties proceeded from one of two causes—either they were under construction involving the raising of large sums before they had begun to earn sufficient income to pay operating expenses; or their income was so depleted by the reduction of rates below a profitable basis that the cost of operation absorbed too large a proportion of their earnings.

The Northern Pacific, which was being built toward the sunset, is an example of the former class. It operated 555 miles to practically nowhere, and had issued $30,780,940 bonds on which it had realized only $22,766,923. It was paying an average of 7-3/10 per cent. on its debt and its earnings from operation in 1874 were only $365,343, or $22,876 more than operating expenses, or about one-tenth as much as the interest on its funded debt. It was only through the process of a receivership and a reorganization, in which the bondholders took preferred stock for their principal and interest, that the work of constructing this great road was continued.

The Erie, that road prolific in lessons of railroad enterprise and financiering, affords a striking example of the second class. But there is no need to drag in over-capitalization to account for its receivership in 1875, which followed "as the night the day" from the business causes revealed in the following table.

Business of the Erie, 1869 to 1875.

Year.	Passenger Mileage (thousands).	Passenger Receipts (thousands).	Per Passenger Mile (cents).	Freight Ton Mileage (thousands).	Freight Receipts (thousands).	Per Ton Mile (cents).
1868–69...	128,455	$4,043	3.15	817,829	$12,583	1.54
1869–70...	133,589	3,968	2.97	898,862	11,983	1.33
1870–71...	148,242	3,972	2.68	897,446	12,861	1.44
1871–72...	156,143	3,329	2.13	965,925	14,509	1.52
1872–73...	164,633	3,651	2.22	1,032,986	15,015	1.45
1873–74...	160,204	3,705	2.31	1,047,420	13,740	1.31
1874–75...	155,396	3,461	2.23	1,016,618	12,287	1.21

The reduction in passenger and freight rates between 1871 and 1875 tells the tale—and it is an old one—of this Erie receivership. If the railroad had received the same rates in 1875 that it did in 1870-71, its receipts from passengers would have been $4,164,612 instead of $3,461,304, and from freight $14,639,299 instead of only $12,287,399.

The same cause—reduced rates—produced the same results throughout the country. The year 1876 showed an increase of 6,092,000 tons of freight moved over the previous year with an absolute decrease of $2,922,858; and Poor's Manual presents the following table showing the conditions prevailing in the three states of Massachusetts, New York and Ohio as illustrative of the effect of reduced rates in New England, the Middle States and the Middle West:

	TONS MOVED.			Rate per Ton Mile in Cents.	
	1876.	1871.	Increase.	1876.	1871.
Massachusetts........	11,327,502	8,934,104	2,393,398	2.04	3.11
New York..........	22,891,828	14,174,544	8,717,284	1.19	1.77
Ohio...............	29,348,788	18,554,340	10,794,459	1.12	1.82
Total............	63,568,129	41,662,988	21,905,141	1.23	1.94

This showed a decrease of .71 of a cent per ton mile for these states—a ratio which, if applied to the whole country, meant that in 1876 the railways received $132,000,000 less than they would have received had the rates of 1871 been in effect.

Evidently it was the **watering of the rates** and not of the capital of the railways that was the "most potent" cause of the receiverships of 1874-1877, involving the following mileage and capital:

INVOLVED IN RECEIVERSHIPS IN 1874-1877.

	Mileage.	Capital Stock.	Funded Debt.
1874	6,825	$235,179,293	$236,285,961
1875	6,280	211,740,414	204,312,038
1876	3,692	87,181,928	114,783,799
1877	3,917	65,454,116	95,937,385
Total	20,714	$599,555,751	$641,319,183
Total Capitalization			$1,140,874,934

As the total operated mileage of the country in 1874 was only 69,273, capitalized at $4,221,763,594, it is evident that two-sevenths of the mileage and more than one-quarter of the capitalization was involved in the financial tribulations of these four years of business stagnation.

Incomplete as are the reports of the cost of construction of these 20,714 miles, they show an aggregate of $1,032,783,972 expended, or within $107,090,962 of the capitalization involved, without counting in the discounts paid to obtain funds in many cases, or the appreciation of much of the property and rights which had accrued during the forty years of railway construction.

Before they were reorganized, the original investment of the stockholders in some of the roads was entirely wiped out, in some it was scaled down and in others, as in the case of the Erie, working capital was obtained by assesments on stockholders. The Northern Pacific emerged from the receivership with its bonded indebtedness and deferred interest converted into preferred stock.

It was not until 1880 that railway earnings showed that they had partially recovered from the severe drag that followed the depression of 1873-74. But so urgent had been the demand for more railways in the meantime that, while the gross earnings increased from $520,466,016 in 1874 to $613,733,610 in 1880, the earnings per mile were still below those of 1874.

A study of the dividends paid during the period of depression reveals how exhausting was the process through which the railways were pumped dry of any water that had been injected into their stock prior to 1871—and even their critics admit that it was comparatively little:

DIVIDENDS DURING DEPRESSION OF 1873.

	Dividends Paid on Stock.	Per Cent on Stock.
1872	$64,418,418	3.91
1873	67,120,709	3.45
1874	67,042,942	3.37
1875	74,294,208	3.38
1876	68,039,668	3.03
1877	58,536,312	2.53
1878	53,629,368	2.34
1879	61,681,470	2.57
1880	77,115,371	2.84

From which it is apparent that the low point in the profits from investments in railway stocks for this period was touched in 1878. There was a further recovery which reached 2.94 per cent. in 1881, but from that year to this dividends on gross capital stock have never risen to the level of 1872, whereas they were destined to go many points lower.

So large a proportion of capital stock in 1876 was non-paying that the dividend rate on paying issues was 7.26 per cent., which it is interesting to compare with the 5.78 per cent. paid on dividend paying stock during the prosperous year 1905.

THE RECESSION OF 1885.

With the return of good times and a sound currency in 1880, there came a resumption of railway building which proved that the country was anxious for more transportation facilities, although in much of the territory into which roads were extended it had not the traffic in sight to support them. In the four years 1880-1883 inclusive, over 31,000 miles were added to the mileage in the United States, being equivalent to an increase of nearly 40 per cent. over the mileage of 1879. Nothing like it had been known before, although it has been equalled since. This phenomenal construction was accompanied by an increase of capitalization amounting to no less than $5,091 per mile, so that in 1883 the gross capitalization of American railways was $64,768 per mile. While much of this increase was through duplication, it has been estimated that $550,000,000 was either wholly fictitious or represented the reckless and sometimes unscrupulous financiering of a period of feverish speculation and over-production. The paralleling of the New York Central by the West Shore, which was scarcely opened for business before it went into a receivership, to be bought for what it was worth under foreclosure by the road it was intended to rival; and the construction of the "Nickel Plate" solely for speculative purposes, were two characteristic incidents of the years preceding the "panic of 1884." Only the excellence of the crops and favorable trade balances tided the country over a universal business catastrophe which was predicted by conservative observers.

Such were the conditions that presaged another period of receiverships for railways in 1884, as shown in the following table:

RECEIVERSHIPS 1880–1885.

Year.	Number of Roads.	Mileage.	Capital Involved.
1880	13	885	$140,265,000
1881	5	110	3,742,000
1882	12	912	39,074,000
1883	11	1,990	108,470,000
1884	36	8,846	669,088,000
1885	46	8,557	466,416,000
1886	12	1,770	67,584,000
1887	10	1,204	92,500,000
Total	145	24,274	$1,587,139,000

During the year 1884 no less than 48 companies operating 15,359 miles of road with an aggregate capitalization of $708,594,046 (exclusive of nearly $100,000,000 funded debt of the Philadelphia & Reading Railroad involved with the Philadelphia & Reading Iron & Coal Company) were in the hands of receivers, against which the construction account showed a cost of $612,419,335, with many omissions.

While a large number of the roads included in the foregoing table were taken out of the hands of the courts through reorganizations, the following statement of the foreclosure sales during the three years 1885-1887 show how the majority of them fared:

Railroad Foreclosure Sales 1885–1887.

Year.	Roads.	Mileage.	Capitalization.
1885	26	2,898	$267,956,000
1886	39	7,858	420,367,000
1887	28	5,129	311,649,000
	93	15,885	$999,972,000

Through these proceedings and the accompanying reorganizations it is estimated that investments in about $500,000,000 par value of capital stock were wiped out. By 1887 the so-called water in American railways had been pretty effectually evaporated; and the track was clear for another period of construction, expansion and competition.

Billions Involved in the Panic of 1893.

Between the years 1877 and 1887, before the Interstate Commerce Act was passed, there had been a remarkable reduction in rates. In the former year, according to Judge Cooley, chairman of the Commission, "the rates charged on first, second, third and fourth classes of freight from New York to Chicago were, respectively, 100, 75, 60 and 45 cents a hundred pounds. They are now (1887) 75, 65, 50 and 35 cents, but the classification as to many articles has in the meantime been reduced so that the actual reduction is greater than these figures would indicate. Rates from Chicago to New York are also proportionately less. A similar result has been apparent elsewhere."

In 1888, at the end of a decade during which freight rates had been reduced fully 25 per cent., the condition of the railways, as summarized from the first reports to the Commission, was as follows:

First Official Railway Statistics, 1888.

Mileage (official) (miles)...	136,883
Locomotives (number)..	29,036
Passenger cars (number)...	25,665
Freight cars (number)...	885,668
Capital stock..$3,864,468,055	
Funded debt.. 3,869,216,365	
Total capital..	$7,733,684,420
Cost of road and equipment (1889)...	7,271,498,570
Passengers carried one mile (number)......................................	10,950,000,000
Average number in a train...	42
Receipts from passengers..	$237,266,377
Revenue per passenger per mile (cents)....................................	2.349
Average cost of carrying one passenger per mile (cents)...................	2.042
Tons of freight carried one mile (number).................................	61,027,000,000
Average haul per ton (miles)..	127.36
Revenue per ton per mile (cents)..	1.001
Average cost of carrying one ton per mile (cents).........................	0.630
Interest on bonds and other debt..	$205,288,021
Dividends paid..	78,943,041
Number of employes (1889)...	704,473
Compensation..	$400,294,024

A comprehension of the items in this table is necessary to an understanding of the causes leading up to the crash of 1893. With the recovery from the recession of 1884, railway building was resumed with a rush, so that in the six years 1887 to 1892, inclusive, no less than 40,803 miles of line or over 30 per cent. was added to the mileage of 1886. Almost as many more miles of subsidiary track was laid during the same period, so that it is not at all surprising to find that by 1892 the gross capitalization had increased to $9,686,146,813, of which, however, $1,391,457,053 was duplicated through intercorporate ownership.

That a large expansion of capital was necessary to meet the demands of traffic is proved by the fact that the passengers caried one mile in 1892 numbered 13,362,898,299, an increase of 30 per cent. over 1888, and the tons of freight caried one mile were 88,241,050,225, an increase of over 44 per cent. during the same period.

An increase of 30 per cent. in passenger service and of 44 per cent. in the freight service performed for the public would appear to justify an addition of 30 per cent. to the mileage constructed by an addition of only 25 per cent. to the gross capitalization, irrespective of how that capitalization was swelled with "water" or intercorporate ownership.

And so in fact it would, but for the undermining effect of the reduction in rates which attended these efforts to keep abreast of the increasing demands for transportation. The following table shows the actual receipts of 1892 from passengers and freight compared with what they would have been had the rates of 1888 been sustained:

	1892. Actual.	1892. On the Rates of 1888.
Gross passenger earnings..........................	$286,805,708	$313,930,500
Gross freight earnings............................	799,316,042	833,392,400
Total..	$1,086,121,750	$1,197,322,900
Loss in revenue due to reduction of rates............................		**$111,201,150**

It only needed another year's continuation of the suicidal policy of rate reduction, coincident with a recession in business, to plunge scores of railroad companies into bankruptcy. And despite the phenomenal passenger traffic of the World's Fair year, the coincidence happened in 1893, although only partially reflected in the official statistics for that year. The full effect of the havoc wrought in railway receipts by a continuous reduction in rates was shown in a "deficit from operations" of $45,851,294 in 1894, where there would have been a surplus of $109,253,085 had the rates of 1888 been maintained.

Commenting on what followed, the Official Statistician said: "Railway construction was arrested, development of railway equipment was nearly stationary, railway employes were reduced and that after a series of years which showed an average annual increase in the payroll of 42,215 employes. * * * Every item on the income account shows a decrease. * * * To meet the deficit occasioned by the payment of the usual dividends to stockholders and to operate the property, it was found necessary to reduce the corporate investments in stocks and bonds by $7,094,413, to reduce the cash and current assets by $44,402,673, and to deplete the fund of materials and supplies so that the stock on hand was worth $13,988,383 less at the close than at the beginning of the year."

As a matter of act, the statistician's own figures show that the usual dividends were not paid to stockholders, being only $95,515,226 on $4,834,075,659 outstanding in 1894 against $100,929,885 on only $4,668,935,418 in 1893. Had the "usual dividends" of 1893 been paid in 1894 they would have been $104,414,000, or nearly $9,000,000 more than they were.

The real reason why the several funds mentioned by Professor Adams had to be reduced or depleted was not the payment of the "usual dividends" or the operation of the property, but the fact that the average passenger receipts had been reduced from 2.349 cents per mile in 1888 to 1.986 cents in 1894 and the average freight receipts had declined from 1.001 cents to 0.860 cents during the same period. The consequent loss in passenger receipts was $51,869,070, and in freight receipts $113,272,350; making a total loss due to this cause alone of $164,142,420.

"This first and most potent cause" resulted in placing 192 roads, with a mileage of 40,818 miles and a capitalization of about $2,500,000,000, under the control of receiverships as of June 30, 1894, which led the statistician to exclaim, "This as a record of insolvency is without a parallel in the previous history of American railways, except it be in the period from 1838 to 1842."

On a preceding page (61) is given a brief table of the receiverships from 1894 to 1899, inclusive, from data supplied by the official reports. Poors' Manual for 1900, in an exhaustive review of the subject, gives a complete list of the roads placed under receiverships and sold under foreclosures during the years 1884 to 1899, inclusive, of which the following are summaries:

SUMMARY BY YEARS OF NUMBER, MILEAGE AND CAPITAL OF
RAILWAYS PLACED IN RECEIVERS' HANDS 1884–1899:

Year.	No.	Mileage.	Stocks.	Bonds.	Total Capitalization.
1884	36	8,846	$270,002,059	$ 399,086,119	$ 669,088,178
1885	46	8,557	248,071,302	218,345,400	466,416,702
1886	12	1,770	31,310,375	36,274,443	67,584,818
1887	10	1,204	48,474,192	44,026,400	92,500,592
1888	21	3,209	106,389,535	93,249,357	199,638,892
1889	21	3,777	100,720,288	94,058,562	194,778,850
1890	21	2,462	44,668,355	59,628,363	104,296,718
1891	30	1,963	47,952,915	30,396,552	78,349,467
1892	40	4,250	196,440,572	143,732,248	340,172,820
1893	119	27,883	835,768,845	1,160,426,166	1,996,195,011
1894	45	4,177	151,036,759	103,779,192	254,815,951
1895	33	3,390	148,966,639	193,631,529	342,598,168
1896	35	2,940	95,207,200	147,929,905	243,137,105
1897	21	1,463	45,891,071	44,624,111	90,515,182
1898	19	2,048	61,415,800	85,287,590	146,703,390
1899	12	1,043	29,676,250	37,401,000	67,077,250
Totals	521	78,582	$2,461,992,157	$2,891,876,937	$5,353,869,094

SUMMARY BY YEARS OF NUMBER, MILEAGE AND CAPITAL OF
RAILWAYS SOLD UNDER FORECLOSURE 1884–1899:

Year.	Number.	Mileage.	Stocks.	Bonds.	Total Capitalization.
1884	16	694	$ 12,924,000	$ 13,061,000	$ 25,985,000
1885	26	2,898	122,280,688	145,676,077	267,956,765
1886	39	7,858	197,744,517	222,623,094	420,367,611
1887	28	5,129	158,722,274	152,926,782	311,649,056
1888	17	1,486	28,793,950	31,568,500	60,362,450
1889	27	2,802	62,464,713	83,456,187	145,920,900
1890	26	3,302	75,998,588	77,994,191	153,992,779
1891	22	3,281	73,483,621	83,190,500	156,674,121
1892	25	1,329	30,758,770	22,446,480	53,205,250
1893	21	1,123	30,974,450	17,791,500	48,765,950
1894	44	5,915	232,272,980	186,332,775	418,605,755
1895	53	10,446	316,723,841	452,095,991	768,819,832
1896	66	12,355	430,195,249	670,800,272	1,100,995,521
1897	42	5,831	239,351,195	201,173,947	440,525,142
1898	43	5,956	104,308,123	123,168,151	227,476,274
1899	28	3,408	117,111,734	147,724,479	264,836,213
	523	73,813	$2,234,108,693	$2,632,029,926	$4,866,138,619

It will be perceived in a study of these two summaries together that scarcely were the railways foreclosed out of their trials, following the panic of 1884, than they were overtaken by the political and industrial storm of 1892-1893.

Among the principal roads included in the above summaries which went into receivers' hands and emerged through foreclosures were the following:

Railroads.	Year of Receivership.	Miles Owned.	Capital Stock.	Bonds.
Atch. Top. & Santa Fe...............	1893	4,438	$102,000,000	$228,082,000
Atlantic & Pacific...................	1894	691	79,760,000	38,913,629
Baltimore & Ohio....................	1896	532	30,000,000	81,251,376
Balt. & Ohio Southwestern...........	1898	921	30,000,000	51,844,690
Chesapeake & Ohio..................	1887	511	36,098,282	32,881,400
Denver & Rio Grande................	1884	1,317	38,000,000	28,123,000
East Tenn., Virginia & Ga. R. R......	1885	1,071	44,000,000	26,200,000
East Tenn., Virginia & Ga. Ry.......	1892	1,265	57,000,000	39,000,000
Missouri, Kansas & Texas............	1888	1,595	46,410,157	46,630,000
New York & New England...........	1884	326	20,000,000	12,833,000
New York & New England...........	1893	361	23,632,000	16,500,000
N. Y., Chicago & St. Louis...........	1885	513	50,000,000	20,046,000
N. Y., L. Erie & Western............	1893	544	86,363,600	77,643,885
N. Y., West Shore & Buffalo.........	1884	473	40,000,000	70,000,000
N. Y., Penn. & Ohio.................	1895	431	44,999,350	96,736,000
Norfolk & Western..................	1895	1,328	59,500,000	55,074,200
Northern Pacific....................	1893	3,429	85,140,131	133,026,000
Oregon Ry. & Navigation Co.........	1893	643	24,000,000	22,703,000
Oregon Short Line..................	1893	1,480	26,161,720	49,832,000
Philadelphia & Reading..............	1884	327	34,668,425	97,782,327
Philadelphia & Reading..............	1893	327	40,426,000	152,000,000
St. Louis & San Francisco...........	1893	992	50,000,000	42,686,300
Union Pacific.......................	1893	1,823	60,868,500	85,492,185
Wabash, St. Louis & Pacific.........	1884	2,483	52,626,800	76,434,834
Wisconsin Central...................	1893	668	14,735,475	18,214,122
St. Louis, Ark. & Texas..............	1889	1,222	23,083,000	32,808,000
Texas & Pacific.....................	1885	1,487	32,164,600	43,340,000
		31,198	$2,131,638,040	1,676,077,948

The potent story—if not the whole story—of what caused most of the 1893 receiverships is told in the decrease in their gross receipts per mile between 1893 and 1894, which was in turn caused by the decline in their average receipts per passenger and ton mile as exhibited in the following table of those roads whose statistics are available:

COMPARATIVE SUMMARY OF EARNINGS PER MILE, AND PER PASSENGER AND TON MILE OF 12 RAILWAYS INVOLVED IN RECEIVERSHIPS 1893–1894.

Road.	1893. YEAR ENDING JUNE 30.			1894. YEAR ENDING JUNE 30.		
	Gross Earnings per Mile.	Receipts per Pas. Mile (cents).	Receipts per Ton Mile (cents).	Gross Earnings per Mile.	Receipts per Pas. Mile (cents).	Receipts per Ton Mile (cents).
A. T. & S. F..........	$5,523	2.264	1.191	$4,521	2.096	1.092
Balt. & Ohio..........	15,230	1.660	.69	12,996	1.590	.670
E. Tenn., Va. & Ga....	4,560	2.400	.85	3,134	2.390	.820
N. Y. & N. England...	11,040	1.990	1.09	9,800	1.970	1.060
N. Y., L. Erie & West..	17,635	1.572	.637	14,819	1.514	.596
Nor. & Western.......	6,447	2.897	.514	6,154	2.850	.466
Northern Pacific......	5,383	2.630	1.230	3,729	2.460	1.120
Ore. Ry. & Nav. Co....	4,560	3.056	1.850	3,650	2.888	1.640
Ore. Short Line.......	5,570	2.603	1.206	4,120	2.481	1.081
Phila. & Reading......	19,503	1.804	1.036	17,360	1.773	1.011
St. Louis & S. Fran....	5,052	2.319	1.198	4,184	2.116	1.126
Union Pacific.........	11,176	2.040	1.060	9,535	1.950	.980

Moreover, the rates for both passengers and freight in 1893 were already almost at the bottom of the gradual decline that brought them from the level of the 1884 period of receiverships to that of the 1894 period. Between these years the rates of the Atchison, Topeka and Santa Fe fell from 2.648 cents per passenger mile and 1.882 cents per ton mile to those given in the above table; of the New York and New England from 2.02 and 1.41 cents respectively; of the New York, Lake Erie and Western (the Erie) from 2.188 and .685 cents; of the Norfolk and Western from 2.71 and 1.18 cents; of the Northern Pacific from 3.44 and 1.96 cents; of the Oregon Railway and Navigation Company from 3.99 and 3.45; of the Philadelphia and Reading from 1.84 and 1.38 cents; of the Union Pacific from 2.903 and 1.910 cents; and of the St. Louis and San Francisco from 2.87 and 1.57 cents.

For the entire country the rates per mile between 1884 and 1894 declined from 2.36 to 1.986 cents per passenger and from 1.13 to 0.86 cents per ton. This decrease of 37/100ths of a cent per passenger mile and 27/100ths per ton mile caused a loss of no less than $299,775,826—on the traffic of 1894—a sum sufficient to have insured the solvency of every road in the United States during that disastrous year.

It was the steady drain of declining rates, and not over-capitalization that was the "potent cause" of the railway receiverships of 1893-1897.

Before the railways recovered from the prostration and exhaustion of this trying period, millions of fresh capital had to be raised to make good the deterioration inseparable from depleted treasuries. This was independent of and in addition to the millions that might have been paid in dividends that were diverted from the pockets of stockholders to maintain the property and keep it in condition to perform its public service, when politics and financial soundness permitted a resumption of national industry.

Let me illustrate this process by a few well-known examples:

Three Examples of Receiverships.
The Atchison, Topeka & Santa Fe.

As shown in the preceding table and paragraphs, the Atchison, Topeka and Santa Fe's failure to meet the interest on its bonds was due to the drop in its revenues following the reduction of its passenger and ton mile rates from 2.648 and 1.882 cents respectively in 1884 to 2,264 and 1.191 cents in 1893.

When it went into the hands of the Court its funded debt was $228,082,000 and its capital stock $102,000,000. When it emerged after foreclosure its funded debt had been scaled down to $162,278,050 and its capital stock increased to $213,468,000. The increase in stock was accounted for by the issue of $111,486,000 preferred stock to the holders of old 2d mortgage bonds, amounting to over $90,000,000, on payment of a 4 per cent. assessment, and as a bonus to holders of the original stock on whom an assessment of $10 a share was levied. As shares in the old company for which par had been originally paid were worth only $13 at the date of reorganization, it required faith to pay the $10 a share assessment necessary to hold on. It was 1899 before a 2½ per cent. dividend was declared on the preferred stock, and 1901 before a 1½ per cent. dividend was paid on common.

For eleven years from 1888 to 1898 all capital stock in the Atchison, which prior to the former date had been a 6 per cent. stock, lay fallow, paying no dividends whatever. And as about $13,000,000 in cash was paid into the treasury for the privilege of retaining it, it is clear that from $70,000,000 to $80,000,000 fairly due the owners of the stock and second mortgage bond holders was either paid in by or retained from them for the benefit of the property. Against this there was an increase in nominal capitalization of less than $46,000,000, the ownership of the property had been consolidated and the road renovated and vastly improved at a cost of over $40,000,000, not represented in capital. It is evident that the water in the Atchison reorganization of 1896 was blood drawn from the body of its stockholders for the benefit of the public.

The Baltimore & Ohio.

The Baltimore and Ohio went into receivers' hands in 1896, owning 532 miles of road with $81,251,000 funded debt, and $30,000,000 capital stock. It came out through a reorganization, without a foreclosure, in 1899 owning 1017 miles of road, with $134,233,350 funded debt and $74,227,767 capital stock. It also owned stocks and bonds with a ledger value of over $10,000,000 and operated 2047 miles of road, which had been practically renewed and re-equipped throughout during the three years it was under the receivership. It is not possible to approximate how much cash went into the property during this period, but there was a hiatus in dividends between 1896 and 1900 that represented more than $7,000,000 loss to shareholders, which was used to fertilize the property. Moreover, when dividends were resumed in 1900 the rate was only 4 per cent. where previous to their discontinuance in 1896 it had been 6. It was 1907 before the dividend rate on common was restored to 6 per cent., that on preferred remaining fixed at 4. Where previous to 1896 the Baltimore and Ohio was paying between 5 and 6 per cent. interest, since the reorganization the rate has been between $3\frac{1}{2}$ and 4. Since 1900 over $100,000,000 stock has been sold at par and the proceeds invested in acquiring auxiliary lines, improvements and equipment necessary to meet the demands of a traffic that has more than trebled in the meantime.

Manifestly the effect of the receivership of 1896 and the reorganization of 1899 was to place the Baltimore and Ohio on a bedrock financial basis.

THE ERIE.

As a final illustration of the economic effect of receiverships upon the capitalization of railways, let us consider the Erie, which from its earliest history has been the sport of adverse circumstances. Chartered as the New York and Erie Railroad in 1832, its construction and success were embarrassed by a provision that it was to be built entirely within the State of New York. After many vicissitudes it was finally completed to Buffalo and extended through New Jersey to Jersey City. Its first experience with receiverships was in 1859, from which it emerged as the Erie Railway. We have already reviewed the causes of its insolvency in 1875. It went into that receivership with a total capitalization of $140,808,724 and was reorganized in 1878 with a capitalization of $151,564,595—the increase being wholly in funded debt on which the interest charge was reduced from 7-64/100 to less than $6\frac{1}{2}$ per cent. The capital stock remained the same, holders being assessed $2 or $3 and $4 or $6 per share on preferred and common stock, respectively—the higher rate receiving a premium in income bonds. The sum thus raised, together with funds from the sale of bonds, amounting to $6,000,000, were put into much needed improvements.

During the fifteen years between the Erie's reorganization in 1878, as the New York, Lake Erie and Western, and the receivership of 1893 no dividends were paid on the $77,837,000 of its common stock, and only 6 per cent. in 1882, '83 and '84, and 3 per cent. in 1892 on its $8,536,600 preferred. Between the receivership of 1875 and that of 1893 the receipts from passengers per mile had declined from 2.220 to 1.572 cents and from freight from 1.208 to 0.637. In short, had the rates of 1875 been charged in 1893 the company's receipts would have been $52,891,000 instead of $29,993,160 on the same volume of traffic, and there would have been no necessity for a receivership.

Between 1878 and 1893 the funded debt had been increased from $66,818,203 to $77,643,885 with no addition to capital stock. The mileage owned, leased and operated had been extended from 957 to 1701 miles; the number of locomotives had increased from 466 to 626, passenger cars from 304 to 590 and freight cars from 11,298 to 12,830, irrespective of their greater average capacity.

When the New York, Lake Erie and Western went into the receiver's hands in 1893, its capital obligations were, common stock, $77,827,000; preferred stock, $8,536,600, and funded debt, $77,643,885, upon which last the annual charges were $4,680,781.

When it emerged as the Erie Railroad in 1895, its capital obligations were: Common stock, $100,000,000; First Preferred, $30,000,000, and funded debt, $102,905,577. Including bonds on properties controlled through ownership of capital stock the funded debt outstanding April 1, 1896, was $126,009,100, upon which the annual interest charge was $5,005,899, or only $325,-118 more than on the smaller debt of 1893. An increase of 258 miles of line owned, and the acquisition of all the stock and bonds of the New York, Pennsylvania and Ohio (from Salamanca, N. Y., to Cleveland and Dayton, Ohio) accounts for the major part of this increase in gross capitalization—the securities owned and pledged under its first consolidation deeds aggregating no less than $64,705,000.

In the process of reorganization the shareholders were called on to pay an assessment amounting to $10,844,370. The holders of common stock had received no dividends between the assessments of 1878 and 1895 and the only payments on preferred were those noted above.

The following statement shows the mileage of the Erie owned, leased and operated before and after the receivership of 1893:

	1893.		1896.	
Title.	Length of Line (Miles).	Total Track (Miles).	Length of Line (Miles).	Total Track (Miles).
Owned...................	551	1,228	1,608	2,709
In fee...................	539	....	792	....
Proprietary roads........	12	....	816	....
Leased...................	551	1,083	277	848
Operated.................	598	977	80	172
Controlled...............	270	393	200	209
Erie System.............	1,970	3,681	2,165	3,938

Between 1873 and 1893 the Erie system had been converted from a 6-foot gauge road laid with 64 to 70 lb. iron rails to a standard 4-ft. 8½ in., gauge road, laid with 56 to 60 lb. steel rails, and before it emerged from the receivership the weight of its steel rails had been increased to 68 to 80 lbs. When the change from iron to steel was begun steel rails cost $120 a ton. The cost of improvements planned in 1873 (most of which were executed out of assessments on stock, sales of bonds and from undivided profits) were estimated at $39,720,000.

The unenviable notoriety attending the financiering of the Erie has overshadowed the streams of money from various sources that, since the time when its first stockholders surrendered half their holdings to induce new subscriptions, down to the present day have been poured into its maintenance and improvement.

The work of making the Erie an easy grade line from Chicago to tidewater has been progressing steadily for years. During the past six years the tractive power of its engines has been increased nearly 60%; and in ten years the capacity of its freight cars has been increased 84%. The combination of these elements has enabled the Erie to increase its average trainload over 80%, but it has yet to pay a dividend on its common stock.

Common Effect of Receiverships.

The experiences of the Atchison, Topeka and Santa Fe; the Baltimore and Ohio, and the Erie, were common to nearly every railway that went to the wall in the panic of 1893. They found themselves carrying traffic at such reduced rates that when the volume of business decreased from 14 to 20 per cent. they were unable to meet their fixed obligations. In the reorganizations of 57 roads between 1884 and 1898, assessments amounting to no less than $87,000,000 on stock and $9,000,000 on bonds were called for from their holders.

In 1895 only 29.94 per cent. of railway stock paid any dividends whatever, the total paid in dividends having shrunk from $100,929,885 in 1893 to $85,287,543 in 1895.

It was 1899 before dividends amounted to over $100,000,000 and 1901 before half of the railway stocks paid any dividends.

The intercorporate ownership of stocks and bonds dropped from $1,563,022,233 in 1893 to $1,447,181,534 in 1895, showing a decrease of over $116,000,000 due to the disposal of such assets to the public at panic prices.

In 1899 when the railways may be said to have emerged from the slough of 1893 their net capitalization was only $51,215 per mile against $52,348 in 1892 before the panic. Such increase as there has been in capitalization since has been due to their strenuous efforts to provide tracks and equipment to handle traffic which has well nigh overwhelmed them—coming so soon after the period of enforced retrenchment.

There has been no watering of stock since 1899—the greater part of the recent issues for improvements, extensions and equipment, being sold at a premium.

XIII

SMALL RETURNS ON RAILWAY INVESTMENTS

While fortunes have been made in the construction and financiering of American railways, their history proves that the returns to investors from their operation have been comparatively less than in any other great industry. In 1840 Mr. T. R. Tanner in his "Canals and Railroads of the United States," with admirable prescience, wrote:

"As facilities of intercourse, the moral effects of the general introduction of railroads and canals can never be duly appreciated. Considered as means of revenue, merely, **it is doubtful whether they can be made to yield an interest equal to that derived from most other investments.** * * * The railroads throughout the country will, no doubt, prove hereafter to be more productive than the canals; though, according to a statement drawn up by Mr. De Geustner, the interest on the capital invested in railroads in the United States in 1839 does not exceed five and a half per cent."

This was written when the average fare per passenger was **five cents per mile** and the average freight rate was **nine cents per ton per mile,** and money in secure investments commanded from **8 to 10 per cent. interest.**

Now let us see what the return has been from the time since we have had comprehensive statistics. Before the period of official data, Poor's Manual affords the following summary of interest and dividends paid on railway capital:

Summary of Rates of Interest and Dividends Paid on Railway Capital—1871–1888.

	Interest. Per Cent on Bonds and Debt.	Dividends. Per Cent on Stock.
1871	No data.	4.19
1872	"	3.91
1873	"	3.45
1874	"	3.37
1875	"	3.38
1876	4.32	3.03
1877	4.39	2.53
1878	4.16	2.34
1879	4.53	2.57
1880	4.00	2.84
1881	4.16	2.94
1882	4.39	2.92
1883	4.58	2.77
1884	4.54	2.48
1885	4.65	2.00
1886	4.53	2.04
1887	4.54	2.18
1888	4.20	1.77

These figures include duplications, both in the capitalization and the returns thereon. Since 1888 the official statistician has presented summaries giving the "average rate paid on dividend paying stock," which, however, is valueless as an indication of the return on capital invested. It is included in the following continuation of the preceding statement for purposes of comparison with the rates based on the official reports and as given in Poor's Manual:

SUMMARY OF RATES OF INTEREST AND DIVIDENDS PAID ON RAILWAY CAPITAL—1888-1905.

Year.	Interest Per Cent on Funded Debt.		Dividends Per Cent on Stock.		Average Rate Paid on Dividend-Paying Stock.
	Poor's Manual.	Official.	Poor's Manual.	Official.	
1889	4.40	4.99	1.79	1.93	5.04
1890	4.27	4.86	1.82	1.99	5.45
1891	4.25	4.54	1.87	2.05	5.07
1892	4.25	4.75	1.93	2.15	5.35
1893	4.31	4.79	1.88	2.16	5.58
1894	4.19	4.72	1.66	1.97	5.40
1895	4.24	4.67	1.58	1.72	5.74
1896	4.45	4.67	1.52	1.67	5.62
1897	4.24	4.70	1.51	1.62	5.43
1898	4.21	4.53	1.71	1.78	5.29
1899	4.26	4.55	1.92	2.01	4.96
1900	4.27	4.48	2.44	2.38	5.23
1901	4.24	4.46	2.65	2.70	5.26
1902	4.10	4.49	2.97	3.08	5.55
1903	4.17	4.41	3.03	3.19	5.70
1904	4.01	4.33	3.31	3.50	6.09
1905	3.79	4.28	3.27	3.63	5.78
1906	3.99	....	3.63	....	....

The discrepancies in the average rates of interest and dividends between the official computation and Poor's Manual confirm rather than lessen the value of these figures as illustrating the fluctuation in the returns on railway capital. One set is based on incomplete returns for the calendar years and the other on well nigh complete returns for the fiscal years. Both columns emphasize the failure of the official "average rate paid on dividend paying stock" to reflect the actual return on railway capital. This is more nearly approached in the following table showing the average rate of net dividends paid on the net capital stock, the data for which has only been available since 1898:

Net Dividends on Net Capital Stock Since 1898.

	Capital Stock Outstanding. Not Duplicated.	Net Dividends.	Average Rate of Net Dividends to Net Capital Stock.
1898	$4,236,404,163	$ 83,995,384	1.98
1899	4,307,513,427	94,273,796	2.19
1900	4,375,360,621	118,624,409	2.71
1901	4,069,898,993	131,626,672	3.23
1902	4,314,055,951	157,215,380	3.64
1903	4,357,235,824	166,176,586	3.81
1904	4,397,040,970	183,754,236	4.20
1905	4,484,504,943	188,175,151	4.19

This table proves that the ratio of dividends to stock as disclosed by the preceding computations, based on gross capital stock and gross dividends, is very much nearer arriving at the true rate of returns on railway capitalization than the "average rate on dividend paying stock," as annually computed by the Official Statistician. It also reflects the fluctuations in such returns, which the Statistician's formula does not, but sometimes actually reverses—vide the returns for 1895 and 1899.

From the above tables it will be seen that the average return on capital invested in American railways in 1905, the most prosperous year for which we have complete official figures, was 4.28 per cent. on funded debt, and 4.19 on capital stock, or 4.25 per cent. on all railway capital.

In 1905 the average interest or dividend paid on all description of capital of the railways of the United Kingdom was 4.05, and this was on a net capitalization per mile over five times greater than that of American railways.

If American railways were over-capitalized in proportion as British railways are, it would take a sum equal to their entire gross receipts in 1905 to pay 4.05 per cent. on the colossal accumulation of expenditures on capital account.

The extreme difference between American and foreign systems of capitalization is summed up in two lines:

	Capital per Mile.	Rate on Capital.	Capital Charge per Mile.
British railways, 1905............	$273,438	4.05	$11,074
American railways, 1905..........	53,328	4.25	2,266

The total earnings from operation of American roads in 1906 were $10,460 per mile, or less by $614 than the capital charge per mile on British railways.

No higher tribute could be paid to the economic soundness of the American railway policy of providing for betterments and a large proportion of improvements out of current income. British railways are staggering to a bitter reckoning under the reverse policy of charging all betterments and improvements to capital account.

A Tail-Piece that Tells its own Tale
(On the Great Northern)

Built 1907   Built 1892
Weight, 195,000 lbs. Cost, $15,750.   Weight. 40,000 lbs. Cost, $5,000.

INDEX.

	Page.
Adams, Henry, on conditions in 1800	30
Adams, Henry C., (official statistician), on balance sheet	60
Adams, Henry C., on possibility of valuation	3
Adams, Henry C., on what constitutes capital	47
Alleghany Portage R. R., cost of	66
Atchison, Topeka & Santa Fe, receivership	167
Australian railways, cost of	111
Baldwin, crippled by panic of 1837	67
Baldwin, locomotives, fast passenger 1848 (Illustration)	68
Baldwin, locomotives in 1861 (Illustration)	80
Baldwin, locomotives in 1906	93
Baldwin, locomotives, output 1856—1860	79
Balance sheet, cost as shown by	88
Balance sheet, what it shows	60
Baltimore & Ohio, breaking ground for	35
Baltimore & Ohio, completed to Wheeling, 1850	43
Baltimore & Ohio, receivership, 1896	168
Belgian railways, cost of	107
Betterments out of profits on Pennsylvania	96
Betterments and improvements out of income	24
Boston and Albany (Western) condition of, in 1851	71
British and American railways compared in 1844	103
British railways, characteristics of	102
British railways, cost of	101
British railways, cost of labor in construction	105
British railways, cost per mile 1850—1905	102
British railways, early	103
British railways, land damages for	103
Callaway, Samuel R., estimate of value of New York Central terminal	115
Camden and Amboy R. R., growth of traffic on	45
Camden and Amboy R. R., cost of	62
Canals, Cooley on inability to compete with railways	33
Canals, early, in the United States	32
Canals, Erie	32
Canals, first preferred to railways	19
Capital, Adams, on what it includes	4, 8, 47
Capital, little relation to rates	6
Capital, account in 1906	52
Capital, and cost by groups	98
Capital, comparative, in 1867	48, 100
Capital, gross, per mile	4, 47, 49
Capital, gross, and per mile 1871 to 1905	49
Capital, how duplicated	51
Capital, net	47
Capital, net per mile of line, 1890 to 1906	51, 53
Capital, net per mile of track, 1889 to 1906	54
Capital, originally included current liabilities	47
Capital, sources of	74, 77
Carroll of Carrollton at breaking ground for B. & O.	35
Cars originally the property of individuals	65
Census of United States, 1830	38
Central Pacific, initial cost of	81
Charleston and Hamburg R. R., cost of	63
Chicago and Alton, capitalization and rates	26

	Page.
Chicago and Northwestern, original project delayed by panic of 1837	151
Chicago and Northwestern, first locomotive arrives by boat	43
Chicago and Rock Island reaches the Mississippi	43
Chicago, Burlington & Quincy opened to Quincy	43
Chicago, Milwaukee & St. Paul, Wisconsin Commission on cost	97
Chicago, Milwaukee & St. Paul, see Racine, Janesville and Mississippi	77
Cheap construction, cost of items in	119
Cincinnati, Union & Ft. Wayne, sources of capital for	76
Cleveland & Pittsburgh, original cost of	74
Cleveland, Columbus & Cincinnati, original cost of	73
Columbia and Philadelphia, cost of	64
Columbus, Piqua & Indiana, sources of capital for	74
Commercial, valuation	11, 138
Comparative capitalization	100
Comparison, value of railways as shown by	9
Conditions in ante-railway times	29
Construction, progressive steps in	43
Construction, cost of, first	58
Construction, cost of and net capitalization, 1890–1906	59
Construction, early, buried in archives	62
Construction, early, previous to 1840	63
Construction, early, in decade 1840—1850	67
Construction, early, in decade 1850—1860	69
Construction, early, in 1860	79
Construction, early, in 1870	80
Construction, early, in 1880	83
Construction, early, in 1890	85
Construction and equipment, cost of in 1906	92, 116
Construction, as shown in balance sheet, cost of	88
Construction, composite examples of typical cost	117, 118
Construction, cost, examples of	116, 120
Cooley, Thomas M., on confusion as to sources of fortunes	27
Cooley, Thomas M., on inability of canals to compete with railways	33
Cooley, Thomas M., on object of regulation	5
Cooper, Peter, designed first American locomotive	35
Cost of transportation in 1800	31
Current liabilities originally included in capital	47
Dana, Charles A., on Southern railways in 1865	79
De Toqueville on America in 1835	31
De Witt Clinton, locomotive of 1831 (Illustration)	39
Difficulties in valuation, Minnesota Commission on	7
Discount on sale of securities legitimate	19
Dividends, average on net capital stock	176
Duplication of capital	51
Early construction, economy of	78
Early construction, not designed for heavy traffic	44
Early New England Railways, cost of	20, 63
Early rates on Pennsylvania	66
Earnings no test of cost	8

INDEX—CONTINUED.

	Page.
Elements in railway valuation, Supreme Court on	5, 7
Employes, pay of Japanese railway	111
Equipment, cost of, as shown in balance sheet	91
Equipment, cost of reproducing	123
Equipment, British and American compared	104
Erie Canal, cost of construction	33
Erie Canal, opened 1826	32
Erie Railroad, opened to Lake Erie	43
Erie Railroad, receivership of 1874	155
Erie Railroad, receivership of 1894	169
Estimates of cost of Western roads	72
European and American railways, cost compared	100
European railways, cost of	100
Expensive construction, example of cost of	119
Farms, increased value of, in fifty years	25
Foreclosures, 1884 to 1899	165
Foreign railways, cost of	100, 101
French railways, cost of	106
Freight cars, cost of modern	126
Freight, cost of moving by team haul	38
Freight, rates allowed by first Pennsylvania charter	37
Freight, receipts per ton mile	4
Freight yard in Chicago, a priceless (Illustration)	128
Freight allowed in charter of Cleveland and Pittsburgh	72
Georgia, history of a state road in	124
German railways, cost of	104
German railways, cost of labor in building	105
Grade crossings, cost of eliminating in Massachusetts	56
Grade crossings, cost of eliminating in New York	57
Gauge change of 1880-1887	85
Half the Union without railways in 1860	80
Harlem Railroad, cost of	64
Highways, cost of country	37
History, value as seen in	9
History of American railways	29
Horse path a feature of early railways	65
Horse power used on early railways	35
Illinois Central, Chicago to Cairo, completed in 1856	43
Improvements charged to operating expenses	25
Improvements, cost of, out of income	23, 97
Improvements, legitimate basis of capitalization	97
Increment, natural and unearned	136
Increase of railways in seven Western states 1870-1890	86
Indian (East) cost of	111
Intangible assets in Texas	115
Intangible value of railways	11
Intercorporate holdings of capital	51
Interest, rate of when railways first built	19
Investment, irrevocable	10
Japanese railways, pay of employes of	111
Japanese railways, cost of	107
Japanese railways, method of ascertaining value of	110
Japanese railways, cost of rolling stock of	108
Japanese railways, price paid by government for	110
Knapp, Chairman M. A., on relation between capital and rates	6
Labor, cost of in construction	105
Labor, cost of in Germany	105
Labor, cost of in Great Britain	105
Labor, cost of in Japan	105
Labor, cost of in United States	111
La Follette, Senator, resolution in re-valuation	3
La Follette, Senator, estimate	13

	Page.
La Follette, Senator, seven billion error	14
La Follette, Senator, error exposed	15
Land, damages in Great Britain	103
Land grants	75
Land represented in capital	76
Land values in large cities	132
Land values per capita	132
Land values per acre by states	130
Locomotives, Baldwin, output 1853-1860	79
Locomotives, Baldwin, weight 1853	79
Locomotives, Baldwin, in 1861	60
Locomotives, contrast in 1876-1906	84
Locomotives, cost of first Stephenson imported	37
Locomotives, cost of modern	124
Locomotives, demonstrated to run on curves	37
Locomotives first used in the United States	34
Locomotives, first arrive in Chicago by boat	43
Locomotives, gold medal winner in 1867 (Illustration)	82
Locomotives, freight in 1844 (Illustration)	67
Locomotives, Mallet compound (Illustration)	93
Locomotives race with a horse	35
Locomotives, weight when first introduced	34
Locomotives, weight now	93
Locomotives, weight in 1855-60	79
Mail train, fast, 80 miles an hour (Illustration)	95
Market value of railways	141
Massachusetts railways, statistics of in 1851	70-71
Mauch Chunk Railroad, cost of	62
Mileage of railways in the United States by states 1841-1906	46
Michigan Central reaches Chicago	43
Michigan's experience with state ownership	153
Minnesota Commission on difficulties of valuation	7
Mohawk and Hudson, initial cost of	64
Mulhall, estimate of cost of French railways	106
Natural increment, railways entitled to	136
New England railway, statistics of in 1851	71
New York railway, statistics of in 1851	70
New York and Albany R. R., original estimates for	64
New York and Hudson River R. R., initial cost of	64
New York Central, terminal rights	115
New Zealand railways, cost of	112
Northern Pacific begun in 1870	84
Northern Pacific, cost of construction	122
Northern Pacific, value of right of way	136
Northern Pacific, receivership of 1874	155
"Old Ironsides" locomotive (Illustration)	40
Panic of 1837	152
Panic of 1857	153
Panic and receiverships of 1873	154
Panic and receiverships of 1885	158
Panic and receiverships of 1893	160
Passenger car, first on Pennsylvania (Illustration)	41
Passenger cars, early cost	65, 72, 73
Passenger cars, cost of modern	124
Passenger cars, 1880 and 1905 (Illustration)	90
Passenger cars, steel (Illustration)	91
Passenger locomotive in 1848 (Illustration)	68
Passenger rates allowed by Cleveland and Pittsburgh charter	72

INDEX—CONTINUED.

	Page.
Passenger receipts per mile	4
Passenger receipts in 1800	31
Passenger receipts on Pennsylvania in 1834	66
Passenger receipts in New England and New York in 1851	70
Passenger receipts on the Erie 1868-1875	156
Passenger receipts 1888	161
Passenger receipts 1905	98
Passenger receipts 1893 and 1894	166
Pennsylvania, early rates on	66
Pennsylvania (Columbia & Philadelphia), initial cost of	64
Pennsylvania (Columbia & Philadelphia), rates under charter	37
Pennsylvania, first locomotive used on (Illustration)	65
Pennsylvania, growth of traffic on	95
Pennsylvania income expended on improvements	96
Philadelphia to Columbia, first charter	36
Philadelphia and Columbia, cost of	64
Philadelphia and Reading, initial cost of	66
Pioneer railways of America	34
Population of United States in 1830	38
Population, density in United States 1830-1906	129
Population, density in Belgium	107
Population, density in France	107
Population, density in Germany	105
Population, density in Great Britain	102
Population, density in Japan	107
Population, increase in seven Western states, 1870-1890	86
Postal cars, cost of early and modern	73, 124
Postal cars, modern (illustration)	124, 125
Present capitalization	47
Present cost of road and equipment	88
Price paid by Japan for private roads	110
Profits, undivided reinvested	21
Profits limited to 25 per cent in one early charter	69
Property, value of all in the United States	144
Property, assessed value for taxation by states	146
Racine, Janesville and Mississippi, original cost of	77
Rails, first laid on wooden stringers	37
Rails, early cost of	69, 71, 72, 73, 82
Rails, steel first introduced and cost	83
Rates, charter on Pennsylvania	37
Rates, charter on Cleveland and Pittsburgh	72
Rates, reasonable, early directors judges of	74
Rates, valuation does not control	3
Reasons for valuation	6
Receiverships, Atchison, Topeka and Sante Fe	167
Receiverships, Baltimore and Ohio	168
Receiverships, effect on railways	151, 171
Receiverships, Erie	155, 169
Receiverships of 1873	84, 154
Receiverships of 1884	158
Receiverships of 1893	61, 160
Receiverships table 1884-1899	164
Regulation, Judge Cooley on object of	5
Relation of capitalization and rates, Chairman Knapp on	6
Reproduction, cost of	10, 114
Reproduction of equipment, cost of	123
Renewals in New England, an early instance of	71
Returns, small, on railway investments	173
Right of way, of early roads, donated	77
Right of way, examples of cost	133
Right of way, present value of	127
Right of way, value of by states	130

	Page.
Right of way, not subject to depreciation	71
Sanborn, Prof. J. B., on land grants	75
Service, public, of railways 1890-1900	87
Shareholders entitled to capitalize profits	21
Shareholders, number of	21
Sources of capital	74, 77
Southern roads during the war	79
Southern roads, cost of 1845	68
Speed of travel in 1800	31
Statistics of railways	161
Steel rails, cost of when first introduced	83
Steel rails, miles of, in 1880	85
Stephenson, George, effect of his inventions	33
Stevens, Colonel John, first advocate of steam railroads in U. S.	36
Stocks and bonds, difference as investments	12
Supreme Court, on elements in railway valuation	5
Taxation, value of railways as shown in	11
Taxation, as a test of value	143
Taxation, assessed value of all property for purposes of	144
Taxation, assessed value of railway property for	146
Team haul, cost of per mile	38
Terminal rights, value of	115
Terminal right of way, value of	131, 135, 136
Texas, intangible assets in	115
Texas railways, value of	8, 147
Toledo, Norwalk and Cleveland, original cost of	73
"Tom Thumb", Peter Cooper's engine (Illustration)	35
Track elevation, cost of in Chicago	57
Track elevation in Chicago (Illustration)	56, 57
Traffic as a measure of value	94
Traffic, growth of, on Pennsylvania	95
Traffic, growth of, on Camden and Amboy	45
Tramway, cost of first	37
Transcontinental line, completed 1869	43
Transportation, cost of, in 1800	31
Travel by railway, in 1834	40
Turnpikes, cost of	38
Typical construction, examples of cost of	117, 118
Union Pacific, initial cost of	81
Union Pacific, conditions under which it was built	82
Unearned increment, none in value of railways	137
Valuation of railways, elements entering into	5, 8
Valuation of railways cannot be based on earnings	8
Valuation of railways, commercial	11, 138
Valuation of railways, market	141
Valuation of railways as shown by taxation	143
Valuation of railways in Texas	8, 146
Water in railway capital defined	17
Wealth of the United States in 1800	31
Wealth, the national, 1906	144
Webster, Daniel, on journey from Washington to Washington, D. C.	32
Wellington, A. M., on what stock represents	20
Western states, railway increase in, 1870-1890	86
Western roads, estimates of cost	72
Wisconsin Commission on expenditures for improvements	97
Wisconsin, wealth of, 1830-1906	136